God's Army

God's
Army

STEPHEN BROOK

CHANNEL 4 BOOKS

First published in 1998 by Channel 4 Books,
an imprint of Macmillan Publishers Ltd,
25 Eccleston Place, London SW1W 9NF
and Basingstoke

Associated companies throughout the world

ISBN 0 7522 1322 9

Text © Stephen Brook 1998

A CIP catalogue record for this book is available from
the British Library.

Commissioning Editor: Charlie Carman
Editors: Mari Roberts and Hazel Orme
Design: Roger Hammond
Colour reproduction by Speedscan Ltd
Printed by New Interlitho Italy

INDIPENDENT IMAGE

This book accompanies the television series *God's Army*
made by Independent Image and Double Exposure for
Channel 4.
Director: Ken Kirby
Producers: David Wickham and Andrew Bethell

Acknowledgements
I received full cooperation in my researches
from the Salvation Army itself, which worked at
a feverish pace to set up the interviews and
visits I sought. In this respect I particularly wish
to thank Captain Bill Cochrane and his
unflappable assistant Carol Kilsby.
Commissioner John Gowans made time to see
me at very short notice, and I am also grateful
to the following officers and 'lay workers' of the
Salvation Army who found time to talk to me,
often at considerable length: Captain Peter
Ayling, Captain Len Ballantine, Captain Steve
Calder, Colonel Douglas Davis, Major Marion
Drew, Lieutenant-Colonel Colin Fairclough,
Major Margaret Halbert, Major Margaret
Hardy, Captain Valerie Hope, Stu Morrison,
Major Ivy Nash, Fiona Nelson, Captains Anne
and John Read, Bram Tout, and Phil Wall.

The production team at Independent
Image, notably David Wickham, Ken Kirby and
Matt Shakespeare, gave me every cooperation
and placed many transcripts and other materials
at my disposal. I particularly wish to thank
Andrew Bethell of Double Exposure, without
whom I might not have found myself engaged
in this fascinating task.

The producers wish to thank Vicki Young and
Charlotte Street.

The publishers would like in addition to thank
Robin Bryant, Lynn Rust and Judith Walker of
the Salvation Army.

Contents

Introduction

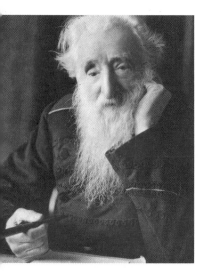

William Booth, founder of the Salvation Army and its first general, in old age, looking every inch the patriarch.

THE SALVATION ARMY, WHICH WAS CREATED in its present form in 1878, has proved a remarkable phenomenon: a church, first and foremost, but one committed to reaching out to the poor, the friendless, the desperate. The Army has been much mocked and caricatured for its military uniforms and brass bands, but it has not faltered in its dedication to what it perceives as its mission. There are no monastic orders within the Salvation Army, and many of its officers put themselves at constant risk in their daily dealings with the alcoholic, the homeless, the prostitute, the addicted. Of course, the Salvation Army is more than a social-welfare agency, even though in Britain it is the most important provider of social services other than the government. As a church, Christian principles underlie all that it does. The primary business of the Salvation Army is the saving of souls, but it has never confined its generosity to those who accept its Christian messages.

This book is a portrait of the Salvation Army at work in Britain today. It looks, of course, at the extraordinary history of the Army and its charismatic founder, William Booth, but it concentrates to a greater extent on the work of its soldiers and officers at all levels: from worship and evangelical work, to social outreach programmes in the inner cities, to the provision of hostels, detoxification centres and other facilities for the homeless, the poor, the elderly and the desperate.

From its earliest days, the Salvation Army has used music to accompany prayer and to win converts.

Age is no barrier to participation in the life of the Salvation Army. An extended family at Kidderminster corps.

Despite the vast number of missions and enterprises undertaken by the Army – and these are multiplied in countless ways in the over one hundred other countries in which it is active – the Salvation Army, like other churches, is in crisis. Recruitment is falling, especially in Europe, and the growing public perception of the Army is that it is outdated and amateurish. The Army's leaders are by no means complacent about this, but there is no consensus about how to turn the situation around. Radical voices, at the very top of the Army as well as among its rank and file, have proposed radical solutions, but there is resistance to anything that will change a much loved organization and its traditions.

This book has no answers to propose, but it will suggest that the survival of the Salvation Army is not merely of interest to its members. Even those out of sympathy with its evangelical message may well take the view that Britain without the Salvation Army would be a poorer and harsher place.

William Booth and his army

WE THINK OF THE VICTORIAN ERA as a God-fearing age, with Gothic revival churches sprouting across our townscapes. In fact, the truth was different. Those who attended church regularly, of whatever the denomination, were outnumbered by those who did not. Moreover, those belonging to the Nonconformist churches were more numerous than those allied to the Church of England.

The lacklustre reputation of the Church of England was, perhaps, not surprising, given its identification with the nation's ruling classes. Agricultural labourers and factory fodder alike found more in common with the fervent preachers of the Nonconformist movements than with the clipped tones and staid rituals of the Anglican clergy. Nonconformist preachers, although in the ascendant, were challenged by the great sea of the religious uncommitted and eagerly set out to save those souls by means of a variety of missions and preaching circuits. It was from this world of religious ardour combating a tide of godless indifference that the Salvation Army sprang.

When William Booth was born, in 1829, Methodism was well established. The third of five children, he grew up in the

Even in old age William Booth was indefatigable, touring Britain, and indeed the world, in order to spread the Gospel.

Nottinghamshire village of Sneinton. Apprenticed to a pawnbroker at the age of thirteen, he soon became aware of the widespread misery and hardship that allowed pawnbrokers to prosper. His own family experienced considerable poverty, since his father died when he was fourteen years old. By this time the youthful William was already quite radical in his politics, and a keen supporter of the reformist movement known as Chartism. Although his family were formally members of the Church of England, he himself was drawn to the Methodists, and attended the Broad Street Wesleyan Chapel in Nottingham.

In 1849 Booth and his sister moved to London to improve their fortunes. Here his radical, reformist zeal put him at odds with the Methodist establishment. Booth bounced from one reformist movement to the next, even spending a few months as an aspiring Congregationalist minister, until in 1854 he settled down with the Methodist New Connexion. Life had not been easy for the impoverished preacher, and he might have had to abandon what he felt to be his calling had it not been for the financial support of a boot retailer called Edward Harris Rabbits.

By this time William Booth was engaged to Catherine Mumford, a young woman in sympathy with his reformist views. They had met when Booth came to preach at her local church at the prompting of Mr Rabbits. In 1852 the couple agreed to marry. Three years passed before they could afford to do so, since after a few months Rabbits had withdrawn his help. The wedding eventually took place on 16 June 1855 in Stockwell. Even on their honeymoon William found time to preach, presumably with his bride's ardent approval. Catherine, who had been born in Ashbourne, Derbyshire, in the same year as her husband, was a formidable woman in her own right, and contributed greatly to the ideological foundations of the Salvation Army. Fiercely feminist in her convictions, Catherine was surely responsible for persuading her husband to allow women to play an equal role in the pursuit of evangelical goals. By the time she was in her teens she had already read the Bible repeatedly, and survived bouts of serious ill-health, including incipient tuberculosis.

Her difficult childhood and teenage years must have toughened her, for she subsequently bore and raised eight children, but she died well before Booth, in October 1890. Like her mother before her, she had had cancer.

In the late 1850s the couple were essentially revivalist preachers and were based at a chapel in Gateshead, but by 1861 the Booths were on the road again, travelling and preaching extensively in the West Country. In 1865 they returned to London and joined the Christian Revival Association. Booth enjoyed some celebrity as a tent preacher in the East End before he set up more permanent headquarters at a theatre in Whitechapel. By the late 1860s his mission was beginning to resemble what would eventually emerge as the Salvation Army. By 1868, his band of preachers had helped to

The Booth family in 1862. From left to right: Kate, William, Emma, Bramwell, Catherine with baby Herbert, and Ballington.

RIVAL SERVICES.
Salem Chapel, Hood Street

WM. BOOTH

Will preach in the Morning at half-past 10, and in the Evening at 6,

On Sunday Next, October 23, 1859,
And every Evening during the Week,
Saturday excepted, at 7 o'Clock.

Many of William Booth's early revivalist services were held at tent meetings in the East End of London.

establish eleven mission halls in the East End and were increasingly involved in social issues, such as poor relief and savings banks. Yet at this stage in his career Booth, however determined, was merely one of dozens of preachers active in the poorer areas of London. However, the influence of his group, now known as the Christian Mission movement, had spread well beyond the confines of East London: by 1877 thirty-one missions were in operation, of which only nine were in the East End. The rapid growth of the movement he led is the best testimony to his extraordinary energy. Although he was of slight build and did not look especially strong, Booth drove himself so hard that an insurance company charged higher premiums than normal for his life insurance, premiums which he willingly paid, and continued to pay, for six decades.

At first Booth had no intention of retaining his converts as members of a church under his own direction. He perceived his job as saving souls that would thereafter be nurtured by the various churches already in existence. Yet at the same time he was developing his own organizational structure, with annual conferences, a monthly magazine, and numerous committees to monitor the growing activities of the mission. The movement attracted finance from different sources. In 1865 one of the Nottingham MPs, Samuel Morley, pledged an annual sum to the Booths; and another philanthropist, Henry Reed, established a trust fund of £5,000, no mean sum.

The Booths' revivalist bent won them little sympathy from either the Anglican or the Methodist establishment. But this became their strength. The working-class poor, who found they had little in common with the established churches, including the Methodists, were more attracted by the Booths' oratory, especially since their religious fervour was matched by social-relief initiatives.

Despite the growing bureaucratic complexity of his burgeoning mission movement, William Booth retained personal control of it, just as he did later of the Salvation Army. This did not make him popular with his colleagues and there were numerous defections. He kept a grip on his growing army of converts, though, by requiring them to sign a pledge modelled on Wesleyan articles of faith.

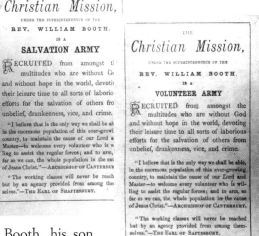

On a momentous day in 1878, William Booth made a crucial correction to a Report of the Christian Mission, and the modern Salvation Army came into existence.

In 1878 the movement transformed itself into the Salvation Army in serendipitous fashion. Booth, his son Bramwell, and his leading associate George Scott Railton were trying to devise a description of the movement's activities. When Railton read out a draft, and came to the words 'The Christian Mission is a Volunteer Army recruited from amongst the multitudes who are without God and without hope in the world', Bramwell objected to the use of 'volunteer', which was also used to describe the precursors of the secular Territorial Army. His father took the pen from Railton's hand, struck out the offending word and replaced it with 'salvation'.

During its early years the Army expanded rapidly. By the end of 1878 there were eighty-one outposts manned by 127 full-time

Despite Catherine Booth's kindly demeanour, she was as determined and hard-working as her husband, and ensured that from the beginning women had equal status with men in the Salvation Army.

evangelists. Of course, the groundwork had already been laid by the Christian Mission movement, with its rigid structure, but Booth, as the Army's general superintendent, planned its campaigns with military precision. Essentially he targeted working-class communities, many of which had been tempted away from their rural parishes by industrial expansion and had in the process lost their religious roots. He also sent his officers into more isolated areas, such as mining or fishing villages. By 1881 the Salvation Army was already installed in its headquarters: a six-storey building in Queen Victoria Street, which remains the site of its offices today.

By 1883 there were an astonishing 519 branches, or 'corps' as they were known, in the Salvation Army. It was increasingly true that officers at overseas corps were locally trained, demonstrating how effective Booth's policy of on-the-spot evangelization had become. Certain features of the Army were not novel, but its use of female officers, often known as Hallelujah Lasses, was innovative and progressive. The military-style organization must also have made an enormous contribution, with sin identified as the enemy and the Salvation Army as a military campaign directed against it. The Army's annual conferences, known as War Congresses, began in 1878. The marching bands, which quickly became one of the Army's emblems, were established in the same year, and songbooks – Booth disliked the word 'hymn', which he considered too churchy – were published from 1883 onwards. Stuffier Christians derided the Salvationists for descending to the level of the music-hall in their effort to gain converts, but the approach was undeniably successful. Along with the bands and songs came the banners, rallies, and uniforms; the famous straw bonnets for women officers – Catherine Booth's idea – were introduced in 1880, and officers were accorded military-style ranks. The most senior officers of the Army were known as Commissioners.

At the head of this rapidly expanding force, of course, was the imposing figure of William Booth. Even during the days of the Christian Mission movement, he had adopted an autocratic stance, which he did not relax. It was ironic that Booth, who in his younger days had experienced such difficulty in accepting more hierarchical church structures such as the Church of England or the Methodists, should himself have developed into a stern disciplinarian. Many who joined the Army found his authoritarianism irksome and unacceptable, but others relished it. However, the organization was hampered by lack of funds, and by 1884 the Army was seriously in debt. It needed money to finance its expansion, and it never came in fast enough, despite Booth's numerous appeals. As he graphically put it: 'We had to build the ship while we were at sea, and not only build the ship but master the laws of navigation.'

Booth set about issuing instructions and orders with alacrity. In 1878, when the Army was still in its infancy, he published *Orders and Regulations for the Salvation Army*, which not only set out its operational standards, but specified the duties of officers and laid down the rules under which they were to conduct their lives. Drinking, smoking, and gambling were forbidden, and officers were only allowed to marry other officers. Further manuals were issued throughout the 1880s, and even the upbringing of children attracted Booth's attention: *The Training of Children* was published in 1888.

Orders and Regulations is an extraordinary document, and marks out Booth as what would today be known as a 'control freak'. The 1925 edition, revised by his son Bramwell, is 565 pages long, and covers in detail such matters as the Army's form of government, financing, the importance of sleep and cleanliness for officers, 'How to Save Sinners', how to deal with 'roughs, toughs, or larrikins', 'the restoration of backsliders', 'how to promote holiness', kneeling during prayer, meetings and ceremonies within the Army, and 'how to resign'. An officer must not only accept decisions made at headquarters, but must do so 'cheerfully'. Officers may not publish songs or books without consent of headquarters, and may not wear jewellery, 'including rings'.

Booth ran a tight ship, and expulsions of officers were common, leading to a high

Pamphlets were sold, giving vivid accounts of the miraculous deeds that result from faith in God.

William Booth and his daughter Evangeline, who would later have an illustrious career developing the Army in North America before eventually becoming General in her own right.

turnover. Nor did he permit any appeal against such dismissals. It was easy to offend: grounds for ejection included frivolous conduct and conversation, marrying a non-officer, the consumption of drink and a refusal to obey orders, and there is evidence to suggest the Army's high command evolved a system of espionage to check on the behaviour of its officers. Those who transgressed were sometimes subject to 'courts martial'. Yet, even within Booth's family there was opposition to his high-handedness, and many of his children, who occupied senior ranks within the Army, chose to resign rather than submit continually to their father's diktats. In 1896 Ballington Booth, his son, set up a rival organization in the United States known as the Volunteers of America, while his daughter Kate also resigned, complaining bitterly that her own attempts at initiatives within her command were being suppressed by her father. Booth responded with the stern words: 'I am your General first and your father afterwards.' Only Bramwell and Evangeline, who ran the show in the United States, remained loyal.

The Army's theological basis was similar to that of Methodism, with an underlying belief in salvation by works as well as by faith. The act of worship itself was typical of revivalist movements, with preaching, prayer, song, and the reading of scripture assuming more importance than any formal order of service. Booth took a relatively undogmatic approach to such matters as the administering of the sacraments and baptism: neither played any part in Salvation Army worship, but there was no anathema against those who wished to participate in the Eucharist. The Army was not unique in its rejection of baptism and the sacraments – both of which had been abandoned long before by the Quakers, who had none the less retained their Christian credentials – and it was eminently user-friendly: all were welcome, there were no reserved pews and no one gave worshippers disapproving looks if they were not dressed in their Sunday best.

As the Salvation Army opened missions throughout the country, especially in the north, the Midlands, and Wales, opposition to its activities grew. The stuffier gentry and Anglican clergy saw it, no doubt correctly, as a threat to privilege and hierarchy, as a force for

The early Salvation Army became involved in practical enterprises that encouraged health and safety. The match factory in Bow, East London, was not, however, a commercial success.

equality that would undermine traditional deference. Opposition took numerous forms but usually consisted of shouting down speakers and pelting them with rotten fruit. But it could also involve physical violence, and many an Army officer was assaulted; in the early 1880s so-called 'Skeleton Armies' were formed to parody the Salvation Army's activities, to ridicule and harass its officers. The Army was not slow to call attention to such incidents in its publications, notably *The War Cry*. (In 1879, Booth had been reluctant to divert his small staff into newspaper-publishing activities, but Bramwell had persuaded him that it would be worthwhile.) Tension was most acute between the Salvation Army and publicans: Booth encouraged his troops to sing their temperance songs and hymns near public houses. There is evidence that brewers, publicans and brothel keepers helped to organize some of the violence directed against the Army. The brewers had close political links with the gentry, so Salvationists could expect little mercy from magistrates when cases involving the Army were brought before them. Moreover, certain local councils sought to ban Sunday processions, although

successive governments tended to override such limitations on freedom of expression. Still, it was not uncommon for officers to be jailed for leading banned processions. In 1884, some 600 Salvation Army members were locked up.

It is possible that the hostility towards the Salvation Army, and the attendant publicity, helped its cause in the long term. It certainly did not inhibit expansion: by 1905 1,116 corps were in operation. In order to focus the officers' energy into expansion, some of the Army's social activities were pared down, such as Sunday schools and soup kitchens. This does not mean that the Army devoted itself exclusively to saving souls and converting the godless: on the contrary, it became involved in such controversial areas as hauling women out of prostitution by opening 'rescue rooms' in areas such as Whitechapel where prostitution was widespread. Some of its ventures in this field were highly controversial: in 1885 the leading journalist W. T. Stead, a close associate of Booth even though Booth disliked him personally, arranged the 'purchase' of a girl called Eliza for five pounds in a bid to bring attention to child prostitution, and to further the Army's campaign for a rise in the age of consent for sexual activity from

Local councils sometimes passed by-laws to prevent Salvationists from preaching and singing in public places. Some Salvationists, such as those shown here in prison uniform, were prepared to defy these by-laws and go to jail.

William Booth, here accompanied by his granddaughter Catherine, made the most of what was then modern technology to tour Britain as part of his mission to save souls.

twelve to sixteen. The girl was well cared for, but Stead and others were prosecuted, and some Salvationists involved in the case were imprisoned for six months.

In 1891 the Army published a volume entitled *In Darkest England, and The Way Out*. Arguing for social reforms, the book was based on the ideas of Frank Smith, one of Booth's closest associates, but ghost-written by W. T. Stead. It argued that high unemployment was directly related to social evils such as heavy drinking and crime – an argument that was still generating controversy a century later – and proposed various schemes to mitigate these evils. The book was amazingly successful and sold 200,000 copies in a year. It was not just a theoretical statement, and the Army went to great lengths to put its ideas into practice. It established a labour bureau, a missing persons' bureau, and a farm where skills in agricultural labour could be acquired. It also offered legal aid to the poor. The following year the

Army took over the running of a match factory in Bow, East London, which allowed it to implement some of Smith's ideas about improving working conditions, pay, and safety in the workplace. As a business enterprise, the match factory was not a success, but it served as a helpful model. Such activities gave an additional dimension to the Army, since they stemmed from religious principle but were not overtly allied to religious dogma. (Some of its enterprises were more mundane: it packaged Triumph, its own blend of tea.) In 1891 Frank Smith decided he could better pursue his ideals via a political forum: he resigned from the Salvation Army and successfully stood for Parliament as a Labour MP.

As the Army gained respectability, it won plaudits from the established Church and from the Methodists and Baptists. A more surprising supporter was Cardinal Manning, the head of the Roman Catholic Church in Britain. The Church of England was uncertain in its response to the militaristic revivalists, but a number of bishops were openly sympathetic to the Salvation Army's aims and activities. Other prominent churchmen, however, were dismayed by Booth's indifference to the administering of sacraments and by the equality granted to women Salvationists. Although there was talk of uniting the Salvation Army with the Church of England, there were too many obstacles on both sides. Booth, for his part, was busily overseeing the expansion of the Army into all corners of the world, and was reluctant to see it too closely identified with the Church of England – which, however, paid him the compliment of stealing his idea in forming its own Church Army.

The Salvation Army had other opponents. The biologist and evolutionist T. H. Huxley launched a fierce attack on Booth and his Army in *The Times*, the basis of his objection being the

William Booth visits Wales in 1907 as part of one of his motorcade tours of Britain.

IN DARKEST ENGLAND, AND THE WAY OUT.

BY GENERAL BOOTH.

WORK FOR ALL

SALVATION ARMY

SOCIAL CAMPAIGN

THE COLONY ACROSS THE SEA

BRITISH COLONIES

FOREIGN LANDS

TO THE COLONY

TO THE COLONY

EMIGRATION FOR DOMESTIC SERVANTS

EMIGRATION IN CANADA, U.S. &c.

EMIGRATION TO ALL PARTS OF THE WORLD

WHITECHAPEL-BY-THE-SEA

CO-OPERATIVE FARMS

CRIME
DRINK
SHAME

DESTITUTI
DESPAIR
DEATH

SUBURBAN VILLAGES 12 MILES FROM TOWN

THE FARM COLONY

SMALL FARM ALLOTMENTS
ACRES AND A COW

PROSTITUTES
In London there are
over 30,000 Prostitutes
In Great Britain 100,000
Privates an Army of probably 100,000
more pure women who devote
increase their earning SHAME

CRIMINAL
In Prison   32,000
Juvenile Thieves   22,000
Reputed known Thieves 32,510
Last year the £
In 500 persons there are

CHAR

DESTITU
In London

THE PO

SALVATION FACTORY

CARP

BUILDING

COBBLING

HOMES FOR

CHILDREN

POOR MANS METROPOLE

HOMES FOR SINGLE

WORKMEN RESTORED
TO MASTERS

TEMPORARY WORK IN
THE COUNTRY

POOR MANS

OAL OFFICERS

MATCH-BOX MAK

CHILDREN RESTORED

BOYS INDUSTRIAL
HOME

BAKERY

BANK

POOR
MANS LAWYER

POVERTY OFFICES

TEMPORARY WORK IN THE
CITY

THE CITY COLONY

WOMENS NIGHT SHELTER

DRINK
Millions of Pounds
The Largest Industry Trade

PREVENTIVE HOME
FOR GIRLS

SHELTERS

LABOUR
BUREAU

SALVAGE BRIGADE

HOMES FOR THE HOMELESS

DRINK TRAFFIC

COMPELLING THEM TO COME IN

RESCUE HOMES

SLUM
CRUSADE

FIRE
FOOD DEPOTS

RED CATE BRIGADE

SALVATION

MISE

THE PO

SUICIDES. 2297
LAST YEAR

FOUND DEAD
LAST

PRISON

WANT

LYING

uncompromising religious ideology that lay behind the Army's charitable endeavours. The great social reformer Lord Shaftesbury even denounced William Booth as the Anti-Christ. When someone commented on the earnestness of the Salvationists, Shaftesbury retorted: 'Was not the Devil himself in earnest?'

In the first decade of the twentieth century, the Army opened corps in Korea, and even penetrated Russia and China. Its overseas activities did not just involve disbursing charitable donations: in India, for example, home industries were established to provide employment for the abjectly poor. Farms and plantations were set up in the southern states, and silk workshops in the Punjab. Leper colonies were founded in Java. In Japan local officers launched a dangerous campaign, at considerable personal risk, to end a system of prostitution that was akin to slavery.

To help furnish the necessary supply of officers, the Staff Training College was founded in Clapton in 1905, the same year that George Bernard Shaw wrote *Major Barbara*, with its Salvationist heroine. By this time William Booth enjoyed the status of a national hero and celebrity. He was not slow to exploit the possibilities offered by that new-fangled invention, the motor car. In 1904 he began the first of his motorized tours of Britain, driving 1,200 miles from Land's End to Aberdeen, visiting sixty-two towns and conducting up to four meetings a day for a month. He repeated such trips six times in the years that followed. Wherever he went he was fêted and received by supportive luminaries such as the Duke of Portland and the novelist Rider Haggard.

In 1907, Booth was received by the monarchs of Denmark, Norway, and Sweden, and collected an honorary doctorate from

Opposite: This chart sought to depict the social mission of the Army worldwide, a mission spelt out in the book *In Darkest England, and The Way Out.*

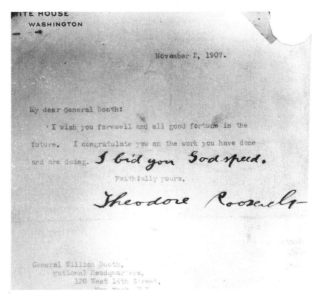

Monarchs and statesmen gave public and personal support to William Booth and the Salvation Army. Here President Theodore Roosevelt bids a personal farewell to the General after his American tour of 1907.

Oxford University. Also that year, when he sailed to the United States, one of his fellow passengers was a future prime minister, Clement Attlee, who recalled him striding ashore with the cry, 'Save your souls, save your souls!' Once he reached Washington, Booth dined with Theodore Roosevelt at the White House, where the president declared himself a great fan of brass bands.

Despite such international celebrity, the Army still endured prosecutions from some hostile local councils. Bangor in Northern Ireland prosecuted a local corps for obstructing the esplanade, and there were similar actions in Widnes, Lancashire, Motherwell in Scotland, and Dartford, Kent. When Salvationists refused to pay their fines, they were often sent to prison. However, the Army made good propaganda use of the prisoners' release, welcoming them home with processions and other festivities.

It was difficult for the Army to keep aloof from politics, since they were inextricably meshed with the social issues to which it was so passionately devoted. In 1908 William Booth came close to issuing a political credo when he told an interviewer from the *Belfast Telegraph*: 'There is a great deal about Socialism that is excellent, but a certain kind of people is wanted to give it effect. Socialism is a celestial system without a celestial people ... If you have got a dirty man and you put a clean shirt on him every morning that will not make him a clean man. It might be favourable to it, but you must change the man and his convictions first; you must get the man himself clean.'

Booth was now an old man, but his energy seemed undiminished. He began the working day at six and often continued until midnight. Whenever he travelled, a portable desk went with him so that his secretaries could type the letters and speeches he dictated as the train rolled on. Yet despite his phenomenal energy, his health, and especially his eyesight, was deteriorating. His last public appearance was in May 1912, when, almost blind, he appeared at a festival of thanksgiving, and told his audience of seven thousand that he was 'going into the dock for repairs'. First, however, he gave one more speech, and his voice filled the vast hall without any amplification.

Death of the General

After William Booth died on 20 August 1912, 65,000 mourners filed past his body as it lay in state. A long procession followed his coffin to the cemetery in Stoke Newington, where Booth and many of the early Salvationists were buried.

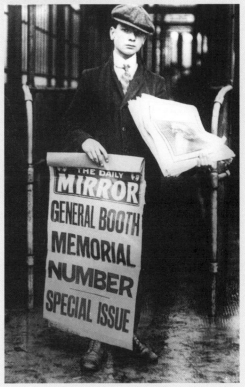

He concluded: 'While there yet remains one dark soul without the light of God, I'll fight – I'll fight to the very end!'

The end, indeed, was near. Later that year, on 20 August 1912, at the age of eighty-three, he died. It is estimated that, during his sixty years as an evangelist he had travelled five million miles and preached sixty thousand sermons. His body lay in state in the Congress Hall, Clapton, and sixty-five thousand people passed by to view it. Queen Mary attended his memorial service incognito.

He was buried on 29 August in Abney Park Cemetery in Stoke Newington in North London, after a four-hour procession. It was announced that his memorial was to be a new training college to be established in Denmark Hill, where it still stands. (Decades passed before the buildings were completed.) Today Booth's grave is flanked by those of other stalwarts of the Salvation Army. His tombstone is in the shape of the Army crest, and the inscription records how he was 'born again of the Spirit' in 1845. His wife, Catherine, is also buried here. Next to his grave is that of George Scott Railton who 'fell at his post, Cologne' in July 1913, and of other commissioners who 'entered into rest' or were 'promoted to glory' or 'left for higher service'. Bramwell Booth and his wife Florence are laid to rest opposite his parents; Florence died in 1957 at the ripe old age of ninety-five. The overgrown cemetery, which is also a nature reserve, is a tranquil and atmospheric place, and it is touching that these doughty warriors for their faith now lie in such a beautiful spot.

William Booth selected his own successor, his son Bramwell, who had for some years been Chief of the Staff. The Army's prestige had never been higher. In 1914 the International Congress at the Royal Albert Hall in London attracted two thousand international delegates, and messages of support were received from President Woodrow Wilson, King George V, and others. General Bramwell Booth led a procession of twelve thousand Salvationists to Hyde Park. By this time the Army was active in fifty-eight countries. There were 9,516 corps and outposts, 16,348 officers and cadets, 1,674 bands and 26,000 bandsmen. It is evident that music-making as a means of saving souls was still considered important: music festivals

A hard act to follow: William Booth with his son Bramwell, who succeeded his father as General and continued the worldwide expansion of the Salvation Army.

were held in the Albert Hall in 1907 and in Scotland in 1911, and tours were often made of European countries. That formidable music critic as well as dramatist George Bernard Shaw wrote favourably about the standards of musicianship.

Under Bramwell's generalship the Army continued to expand across Africa, eastern Europe, and into the Far East. His success was all the more remarkable given his deafness. He also coped well with the tricky task of keeping the movement whole during the First World War, when he resisted the temptation to think of foreigners as 'the enemy'. It was not easy to maintain the international network of which the Army now consisted, nor to deal with the innumerable emergencies that confronted its soldiers in all of the countries afflicted by war. Bramwell had to tread a difficult line, and did so with considerable skill, as when in November 1914 he wrote in the Army's now ironically entitled newspaper *The War Cry*: 'In the name of the God of love, we must refuse the awful demands which are being made by the god of war to yield to the rage and hate and lust of revenge which are only too awfully manifest around us. We must, by the help of God, keep our tender sympathy with the suffering, for it is the sympathy of Christ.' In 1915, he declared: 'Every land is my Fatherland, for all lands are my Father's.' When *The War Cry* published casualty lists of wounded or dead Salvationists, it did not hesitate to include the names of Germans. Needless to say, such an attitude did not win Bramwell many friends at the War Office. Yet Salvationists were close to the battlefield, maintaining ambulances and canteens, usually under difficult and dangerous conditions.

When peace returned, Bramwell, with Florence at his side, travelled widely, establishing a pattern that would be maintained by every succeeding general. Long before popes made a habit of visiting their flock worldwide, Salvation Army generals were undertaking epic journeys to keep in contact with the innumerable corps developing in countless nations. In many ways, Bramwell shaped the modern officer corps, introducing salaries, pensions and children's allowances, and worked as hard as his father had to maintain contact with his officers and his increasingly complex organization.

Raised within the heart of the Salvation Army, Bramwell was unable to see that the system of command and administration devised by his charismatic father might need reform fifty years after its creation. When asked by a journalist whether the autocratic structure of the Army would remain in place, Bramwell replied, with a certain complacency: 'I have no doubt that the military system will be maintained. But those critics who talk of autocracy do not realize that it is an autocracy modified by the system being spread throughout all grades of rank from top to bottom. It is indeed true to say that the greatest victories have been obtained in reality as the result of its application on the lower rungs rather than on the highest rungs of the ladder. It is the sense of individual responsibility animating the simple bandmaster, and the officer with a handful of men, which has brought out so many heroic workers from the depths. This individual command rising through all stages, and this unswerving obedience to the next in command, gives a tremendous cohesion, simplicity, and power to the whole organization.'

By the late 1920s, however, Bramwell was in poor health. His sister Evangeline was keen for Bramwell to relinquish the principle of appointing his own successor and to substitute election. In 1927 she prepared a memorandum recommending these changes but Bramwell wouldn't hear of it. With half the Army's property now located in the United States, American Salvationists were out of sympathy with the autocratic structure of the organization, and she was simply voicing a widely held view. 'Your suggestion,' he replied, 'aims at cancelling the General's most urgent duty – his duty to discern and name his successor; and it aims at this for no useful purpose, for if the named successor be a person whom the Commissioners generally consider to be fit for the office, why interfere? If, on the other hand, after due consideration and trial he be found unfit by the Commissioners, they already have the power of deposing him and electing a fit person in his place.'

THE FOUNDER SPEAKS AGAIN

A Selection of the Writings of WILLIAM BOOTH

Throughout his long life, William Booth's sermons and addresses were collected and published in various formats, spreading the word both to the faithful and to potential converts.

In 1934 Commissioner Evangeline Booth, after a lengthy career heading the Army in North America, was elected General.

By January 1929 Bramwell Booth was very ill, and a High Council, the most senior international body in the Salvation Army and the equivalent of a conclave of cardinals within the Catholic Church, proposed that he 'should retire from office, retaining the title of general and continuing to enjoy the honours and dignities of the same'. Bramwell wouldn't budge and was convinced he would recover both his health and his authority. The High Council persisted, and voted by fifty-five to eight to end his term of active service. Bramwell's lawyers took the matter to court, but in mid-February the High Council again voted that he should retire on grounds of ill-health. Having passed that resolution, it then set about electing a successor. Commissioner Edward John Higgins, already Chief of the Staff, was chosen by a majority of forty-two to seventeen. Bramwell lingered for a few more months and died on 6 June 1929.

Higgins had won the election on a reformist platform, and the changes were brought into effect with the Salvation Army Act of 1931. It placed the Army's property and assets into a trustee company, and put an end to the practice whereby the General named his successor. Parliament felt that the question of the General's retirement age was a matter for the Army to resolve on its own, and it was fixed at seventy. The provisions of the 1931 Act still apply to the functioning of the Army, and are from time to time amended. A tinkering with the retirement age took place in 1975, when the then General, Clarence Wiseman, secured the commissioners' support to lower it to sixty-eight, or after five years' service, whichever should arise first, and it has since been lowered to sixty-five.

These were not the easiest times for the Salvation Army. It had suffered – what had not? – from the Wall Street crash of 1929 and the economic depression that followed. Some branches and colleges shut their doors, and the Army's resources dwindled at a time when the need was greatest. Yet it continued its work and still managed to expand the overall numbers of corps and officers worldwide.

Edward Higgins retired in 1934 and was succeeded by the venerable Evangeline Cory Booth, who had spent most of her Army career in the United States and at one point had been awarded a ticker-tape parade by New York's flamboyant Mayor La Guardia. She maintained her father's tradition of travelling extensively, visiting Australia, California, Scandinavia and other countries within a single year. She oversaw relief efforts during the Spanish Civil War, arranging for 1,400 Basque children to come to Britain in 1937, then returning them to their homeland a year later. George Bernard Shaw was among the many individuals who contributed to the cost of this operation. In 1938 she established the Army's international youth movement with the avowed aim of recruiting young people.

Evangeline Booth retired in 1939, and lived on until 1950. She was succeeded by Commissioner George Lyndon Carpenter of

In 1943 daylight bombing raids caused death and destruction in many parts of England. The Salvation Army was often on hand to give support and refreshment to rescue workers.

The Army and the war

During the Second World War the Salvation Army assisted the needy in numerous ways: ministering to bombed-out families, passing out refreshments in underground shelters, and holding services in caves such as those in Chislehurst, Kent, that served as shelters.

Australia, who took over soon after the Second World War broke out. The Army rose splendidly to the crisis of war: its mobile canteens soon became a familiar sight at bomb-sites and other disaster areas, and its soldiers comforted those who had lost their homes or relatives or who were forced to spend their nights in grim underground shelters. It maintained its efforts in spite of losing much of its property during the war: its headquarters in Queen Victoria Street in the City of London was destroyed, as were its insurance society and a number of hostels and local corps halls.

War involved frustration, as well as hardship, for the Army. Its internationalist instincts had to be put aside as a consequence of the difficulty, in some cases the impossibility, of travel. Also, it had to pursue the morally ambiguous policy of not overtly favouring the victory of either side. This is not to say that the Army behaved in an unpatriotic manner: it merely affirmed that the will of the Lord would prevail – and, no doubt, privately beseeched the Lord to prevail on the side of Britain and its allies.

In Germany the activities of the Salvation Army had been severely restricted by the Nazis since 1937. As in Britain, many of its properties were damaged or destroyed during the war. Afterwards the German Heilsarmee, as it was known, was revived, but a year passed by before contact was resumed with the Japanese Salvation Army. Because of the war, General Carpenter's term of office had been extended but in 1946 he retired and was replaced by Commander Albert Orsborn. At his retirement in 1954, Wilfred Kitching was elected as General, and was succeeded in 1963 by Frederick Coutts.

It was in 1963, too, that the International Headquarters in Queen Victoria Street was at last reopened. After the sleepy 1950s, the 1960s proved more eventful and controversial, and youth rebellion, whether in the form of music, poetry or political protest, became the order of the day. Even the Salvation Army found itself embroiled in controversy. In 1964, embracing the exuberant spirit of the age, Peter

Opposite: A wartime demolition worker, having salvaged a violin, entertains his fellow rescuers while the Salvation Army canteen dispenses mugs of tea.

During the constant stress of wartime conditions, Salvationists put their religious faith into action by offering practical assistance and moral support.

and Sylvia Dalziel, Joy Webb and other cadets from the training college formed a skiffle group called the Joy Strings, which despite its evangelical message proved remarkably popular. Their hits included 'Have Faith in God', 'Follow', and 'Something to Live For Now'. But the Joy Strings attracted the wrath of Billy Graham and other sterner evangelists after they appeared at London's Playboy Club. Yet Graham had misjudged the situation: the Army was more than used to penetrating pubs, the lair of the enemy, and weathered the moral turpitude of a nightclub without being corrupted. The Army took up the cudgels again in 1970, when Gilbert Abadie, the territorial commander in France, protested against the musical *Hair*, which contained not only scenes of nudity but what was described as an 'indecent profaning of the Cross'. French Salvationists marched through the streets of Paris, but *Hair* played on.

In 1965 the Army celebrated its centenary – although this was stretching the historical record somewhat. It was in fact the centenary of William Booth's emergence as a dedicated evangelist in London through his Christian Mission movement, but it could be plausibly argued that the foundations of what became the Salvation Army were laid in that year. The celebrations took place the world over. In Britain the Queen and the Archbishop of Canterbury were among those who gathered in the Royal Albert Hall to mark the event. At the same time the Army was continuing with its numerous international projects, opening clinics and dispensaries in India and the Congo, offering earthquake relief in Chile and flood relief in India, as well as providing food to Ghana and Kenya and various Caribbean countries.

In 1965 the Salvation Army also launched a campaign it called 'For God's Sake Care'. This aimed to create purpose-designed hostels to replace shelters for the homeless and for men sleeping rough. There would be a constant tension between the desire to provide clean, modest accommodation for the homeless and the wish not to institutionalize those who had never been able, for economic or psychiatric reasons, to live on their own. A further study of homelessness was initiated in 1988, when the Army published a report called *Faces of Homelessness*, which came up with useful statistical data that helped to reshape the Army's efforts to combat homelessness. As a consequence it has set up not only hostels for the homeless, but training and detoxification centres, too.

Meanwhile, there was a succession of changes at the top. In 1969 Erik Wickberg was elected General. Although Swedish by birth, he spoke English fluently. He was succeeded in 1974 by a Canadian from Newfoundland, Clarence Wiseman. Three years later Arnold Brown took over. These recent decades have not been easy ones for the Army, which has had to face the dilemma of numerical decline: in 1965 *The War Cry* celebrated the graduation of 142 cadets from the training college at Denmark Hill, but by the late 1990s that figure had dropped to below thirty.

The modern Salvation Army is a vast international organization, with representatives in over a hundred countries. Within Britain it is separated into eighteen divisions under the overall direction of the territorial commander. Its headquarters, both national and international, remain in Queen Victoria Street, in faceless office buildings, but the general public can get to know the Army and its work better at its branch offices in Judd Street, just south of King's Cross. Here, a large bookshop sells the Army's numerous publications, songbooks and recordings, as well as books and pamphlets on spiritual subjects. Attached to it is another shop with uniforms and other Salvationist accessories. Officers and soldiers are required to pay for their own uniforms. At Judd Street you can also find the small museum and archives, known as the Heritage Centre, devoted to the history of the Army. Showcases display rare letters and documents from the early days of the Salvation Army, as well as the uniforms of various periods and other memorabilia.

In the early 1990s the public image of the Salvation Army was dented when it was revealed that the organization, which is, of course, a charity, had been defrauded of large sums of money. A two-month investigation took place, and the Charity Commission also launched its own investigation. An officer at the London head-quarters, Lieutenant Colonel Grenville Burn, had become friendly with a businessman, Stuart Ford, who had offered to help with fundraising for the Army. Ford suggested to Burn that the Salvation Army invest in a money-market scheme that promised high returns. Although the Army's financial advisers warned against it, Burn went ahead. A short while later the funds invested, some £6.2 million, were transferred to a bank in Luxembourg and the Salvation Army lost control of it.

In February 1993 the Army took legal action through the High Court against Ford and an Egyptian businessman also involved in the scheme, and eventually the money was recovered. In April, General Eva Burrows sacked Burn on the grounds that he took unauthorized action without consulting his superiors. At the same time, Territorial Commander John Larsson and his Chief Secretary, Ian Cutmore, were given new jobs. John Larsson is now territorial commander in Sweden.

The present General, Paul A. Rader, an American, commands 17,470 serving officers (1,668 in Britain) plus 8,075 retired officers. Worldwide there are nearly 16,000 corps and outposts, and over a million soldiers and adherents. In Britain alone there are almost 5,000 employees. Among the social-service centres operated by the Salvation Army in Britain are old people's homes, fifty hostels for the homeless accommodating 3,355 people, prison chaplaincies, centres for those with learning difficulties, and a family tracing service. The structure of the Army has not changed greatly since its early years: military ranks are still used, rising from lieutenant to major according to length of service. Senior ranks, from lieutenant colonel through colonel to commissioner, are awarded according to responsibility and are unrelated to length of service. All commissioners automatically become members of the Army's supreme body, the High Council.

Despite the various problems the Army has encountered, it has never neglected what it sees as its international responsibilities. In 1996 its operations included disaster relief after the Port Arthur

When young Salvation Army cadets formed an evangelical skiffle group called the Joy Strings, some Salvationists disapproved of this alliance with popular culture, but the group proved a success with the public.

shooting in Tasmania and after flooding in the Edenvale Valley in South Africa; and it sent clothes to Bosnia and to Yunan, which had been devastated by an earthquake. Strenuous efforts are being made to encourage new corps in Russia and other countries that were once in the Soviet bloc. Around the world the Army operates hundreds of clinics and dispensaries, thousands of schools, institutes for the blind, convalescent homes, 674 old people's homes, 189 children's homes and 778 hostels for the homeless.

Yet, even within Europe there are countries where the Salvation Army is still struggling to establish a foothold. In 1995 a young Greek, who had supported himself and his family by working as a caretaker at Regent Hall (the Army's best-known corps in London), entered the training college at Denmark Hill. He was followed by Polis and Maria Pantelides, who are now second-year cadets at Denmark Hill. Until very recently there had been no Greek officers, and the International Headquarters of the Salvation Army, preoccupied with revitalizing Russian and eastern Europe, did not seem interested in giving Greece a high priority. Now, though, the new Greek contingent hopes to establish a corps and outreach programme in their homeland, especially among refugees from Albania. The Orthodox Church has never been keen to see the Salvation Army – or, indeed, any of the Protestant churches – at work in Greece, but they seem likely to succeed, and the Salvation Army will then have brought its mission to yet another new country.

That mission remains encapsulated, as it has been from the beginning, in the words: 'With heart to God and hand to man.'

The present head of the Salvation Army, General Paul A. Rader of the United States, and his wife, Commissioner Kay Rader.

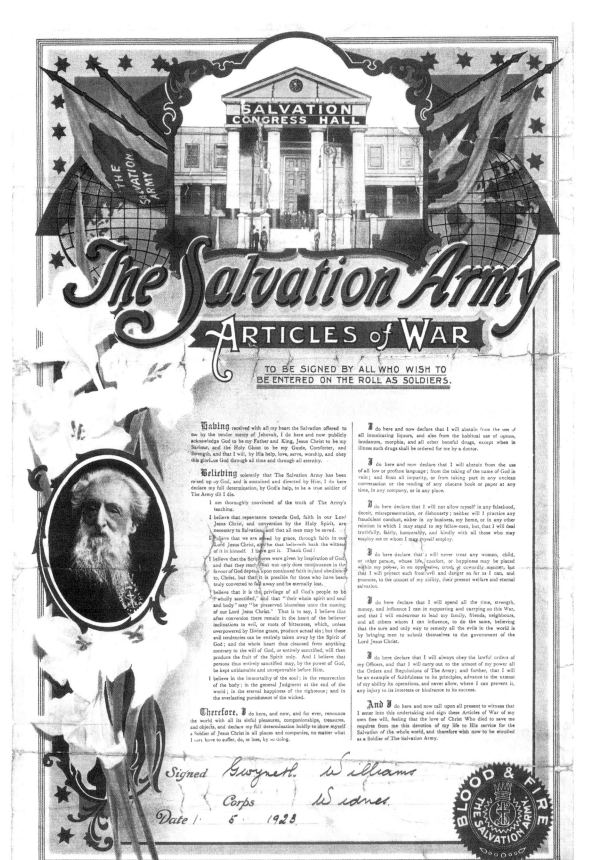

SALVATION CONGRESS HALL

The Salvation Army
ARTICLES of WAR

TO BE SIGNED BY ALL WHO WISH TO BE ENTERED ON THE ROLL AS SOLDIERS.

Having received with all my heart the Salvation offered to me by the tender mercy of Jehovah, I do here and now publicly acknowledge God to be my Father and King, Jesus Christ to be my Saviour, and the Holy Ghost to be my Guide, Comforter, and Strength, and that I will, by His help, love, serve, worship, and obey this glorious God through all time and through all eternity.

Believing solemnly that The Salvation Army has been raised up by God, and is sustained and directed by Him, I do here declare my full determination, by God's help, to be a true soldier of The Army till I die.

I am thoroughly convinced of the truth of The Army's teaching.

I believe that repentance towards God, faith in our Lord Jesus Christ, and conversion by the Holy Spirit, are necessary to Salvation, and that all men may be saved.

I believe that we are saved by grace, through faith in our Lord Jesus Christ, and he that believeth hath the witness of it in himself. I have got it. Thank God!

I believe that the Scriptures were given by inspiration of God, and that they teach that not only does continuance in the favour of God depend upon continued faith in and obedience to Christ, but that it is possible for those who have been truly converted to fall away and be eternally lost.

I believe that it is the privilege of all God's people to be "wholly sanctified," and that "their whole spirit and soul and body" may "be preserved blameless unto the coming of our Lord Jesus Christ." That is to say, I believe that after conversion there remain in the heart of the believer inclinations to evil, or roots of bitterness, which, unless overpowered by Divine grace, produce actual sin; but these evil tendencies can be entirely taken away by the Spirit of God; and the whole heart thus cleansed from anything contrary to the will of God, or entirely sanctified, will then produce the fruit of the Spirit only. And I believe that persons thus entirely sanctified may, by the power of God, be kept unblamable and unreprovable before Him.

I believe in the immortality of the soul; in the resurrection of the body; in the general Judgment at the end of the world; in the eternal happiness of the righteous; and in the everlasting punishment of the wicked.

Therefore, I do here, and now, and for ever, renounce the world with all its sinful pleasures, companionships, treasures, and objects, and declare my full determination boldly to show myself a Soldier of Jesus Christ in all places and companies, no matter what I may have to suffer, do, or lose, by so doing.

I do here and now declare that I will abstain from the use of all intoxicating liquors, and also from the habitual use of opium, laudanum, morphia, and all other baneful drugs, except when in illness such drugs shall be ordered for me by a doctor.

I do here and now declare that I will abstain from the use of all low or profane language; from the taking of the name of God in vain; and from all impurity, or from taking part in any unclean conversation or the reading of any obscene book or paper at any time, in any company, or in any place.

I do here declare that I will not allow myself in any falsehood, deceit, misrepresentation, or dishonesty; neither will I practice any fraudulent conduct, either in my business, my home, or in any other relation in which I may stand to my fellow-men, but that I will deal truthfully, fairly, honourably, and kindly with all those who may employ me or whom I may myself employ.

I do here declare that I will never treat any woman, child, or other person, whose life, comfort, or happiness may be placed within my power, in an oppressive, cruel, or cowardly manner, but that I will protect such from evil and danger so far as I can, and promote, to the utmost of my ability, their present welfare and eternal salvation.

I do here declare that I will spend all the time, strength, money, and influence I can in supporting and carrying on this War, and that I will endeavour to lead my family, friends, neighbours, and all others whom I can influence, to do the same, believing that the sure and only way to remedy all the evils in the world is by bringing men to submit themselves to the government of the Lord Jesus Christ.

I do here declare that I will always obey the lawful orders of my Officers, and that I will carry out to the utmost of my power all the Orders and Regulations of The Army; and further, that I will be an example of faithfulness to its principles, advance to the utmost of my ability its operations, and never allow, where I can prevent it, any injury to its interests or hindrance to its success.

And I do here and now call upon all present to witness that I enter into this undertaking and sign these Articles of War of my own free will, feeling that the love of Christ Who died to save me requires from me this devotion of my life to His service for the Salvation of the whole world, and therefore wish now to be enrolled as a Soldier of The Salvation Army.

Signed *Gwyneth Williams*

Corps *Widnes*

Date *5 1923*

BLOOD & FIRE
THE SALVATION ARMY

2

Beliefs and practices

IN ITS THEOLOGY, THE SALVATIONIST FAITH does not differ significantly from Methodism, in which it has its roots. There is the same emphasis on personal holiness, on personal salvation. The underlying belief is in salvation by faith and good works. The Army's eleven articles of faith, known as the 'Articles of War', are modelled on the Methodist credo. Converts are required to affirm that the Bible is the inspired word of God, and that Christ is both God and Man, that salvation is won by repentance and faith, and that the immortal soul is either rewarded with the infinity of heaven or with eternal punishment in hell. The Army has never been Calvinist and in 1873 explicitly criticized those who sought to deny the existence of free will.

However, Salvationists enjoy a great deal of leeway in the diversity of their ministry. As Captain Bill Cochrane, the external relations officer of the Army, puts it: 'There is no thought police in the Salvation Army.' True, there are the eleven articles of faith, which all new Salvationists must affirm, but they are broad enough to allow considerable latitude. Thus the articles imply some belief in Satanic forces, but how those forces are expressed in terms of the ministry

Soldiers joining the Salvation Army still sign the credo known as the 'Articles of War'. Its eleven articles pledge the soldiers to Christian beliefs and a Christian way of life.

will vary from those who urge the need for constant spiritual battle against the daily intervention of Satan, to those who believe, in effect, in a social gospel in which evil is an expression of social disharmony. Nor is there any uniformity of belief in notions such as the afterlife, any more than there are in other churches: on the contrary, a wide range of interpretations from the literalist to the psychological are tolerated. As for heaven and hell, it is up to the individual to give their own gloss to the belief in 'the eternal happiness of the righteous and the endless punishment of the wicked', as stated in the Army's list of doctrines.

Some Salvationists are born into the faith and the church, others are converted into it, and others drift in from other churches. Brenda Neale, now a cadet at the Salvation Army training college, is perhaps typical of the latter. She had enjoyed a conventional Christian upbringing and faith from an early age. 'Unlike many people today, the idea of sin was something that I accepted, there was evil in the world. This is a society where sin is not recognized, almost anything goes, and if people don't recognize sin, they don't recognize judgement and the need to do anything about sin. That is what the church is all about: showing people that there is sin and what we should be doing about it.'

She worshipped at various churches until one day she walked into a Salvation Army hall in Edinburgh. 'I walked in there and I knew this was where God wanted me to be. I was met with a lot of love and total acceptance. I went along to what were called recruits classes where you basically learn about the Salvation Army beliefs and doctrines and I eventually decided that to be a soldier – a full member of the Army – was for me. Everything I do, everything I'm part of, is influenced by the relationship I have with Jesus as a Christian. So it's of fundamental importance to me.'

One feature common to all Army churches is the mercy seat, which is usually a bench towards the front of the hall. Towards the end of a service, members of the congregation are invited to come forward, which they do for a variety of reasons: a wish to accept the Christian faith, to pray in the company of a sympathetic Salvationist, or to reflect on their spiritual condition or spiritual need. When anyone comes forward to kneel at the mercy seat, an officer or other Salvationist will kneel beside them and offer prayer, consolation, or solidarity. Sermons are central to the Salvationist act of worship. Preaching the gospel, whether to the faithful or to those outside the family of the church, is a large part of what the Salvation Army is all about. However, the stereotype of a 'Sarah Brown' haranguing the godless, as portrayed in the irresistible *Guys and Dolls*, bears little resemblance to the ardent yet gentle style that most officers adopt.

Most Salvationists would probably reject the suggestion that they believe in the literal truth of such Biblical stories as the Creation or the Flood. All that the Army doctrines commit members to is the following: 'We believe that the scriptures of the Old and New Testaments were given by inspiration of God, and that they only constitute the Divine rule of Christian faith and practice.' Salvationists also believe in the Trinity, the doctrine of the Fall, the immortality of the soul and that repentance is necessary to salvation.

Phil Wall, an ardent evangelist and leader of the Army's Mission Team, admits there is great diversity of belief within the Salvation Army. He believes in the authority of the Bible as God's inspired word and as a historical document, but for him the Bible is a mixture of poetry, narrative and prophecy and is literally true only in parts. 'You have to use your brain to work out what is poetry or prophecy rather than historical narrative. But nevertheless that doesn't stop me from believing that the Bible consistently speaks the truth. I think it is the case that, traditionally, Salvationists have not been great theologians. We speak to God more with our hearts than with our minds. The Salvation Army was not set up to be a new church, but to reach people that other churches wouldn't go near. I accept that there is a need within the Army to think better and harder about our faith, to have a mind on fire, a zeal for understanding. I'm not an enthusiast for liberal theology. I don't adopt an empirical approach, a shallow rationalism that excludes the supernatural. I agree that primarily we must *experience* our faith, and this is the Salvationist approach, but for me that's not enough.'

Almost without exception, active Salvationists will insist that the wellspring of all their actions in the community is deep Christian belief. A Scots cadet at the Salvation Army training school, Martin Neale, expressed this view: 'We are a church, we are first and foremost a fellowship of Christian believers who are giving service in the community, through social work, through feeding schemes, through whatever the Army requires. But the motivation is not just about doing good. It's a spiritual motivation. It's through our knowledge of the Word of God that we feel compelled to serve other people. I'm saddened when one comes across those who do not even know the Salvation Army is a church. I'm not suggesting that we cut out or reduce any of our social activities, but what I am saying is that my priority must be the love of Jesus Christ and that my service must be rooted in what Jesus would have done. In meeting social needs, as we seek to do, we as Salvationists must always ensure that our work is motivated in God. We can draw alongside someone and bind their wounds, we can feed them, but we can also offer them that which is spiritual, which in the long term will sustain them. We need more witnesses for Jesus, people telling the world about Jesus and about having a love for Jesus. Ours is a gospel of love.'

For Martin Neale and others in the Army, materialism is the great enemy: 'Materialism provides so much of a crutch that even we, as Salvationists, can come to be so comfortable, materially, that we're not driven to our knees enough, we're not humbled enough, we don't seem to need God in our lives as much as we used to. I'm very much aware of forces leaving us in some areas, some parts of the world, but I also recognize that there's a strong nucleus of empowered people, people who are really filled with the Holy Spirit, and that is the source of power. It's not just a belief in God, it's an empowerment by the Holy Spirit in what we do and how we express ourselves.'

From time to time the Army issues 'positional statements' on topical moral or ethical issues. They are released on the authority of the General and thus represent the view of the Army on the issues under consideration. However, they are not binding on its members, although in practice the great majority would share the views expressed in them. In 1990 the Army published a statement on abortion, supporting the protection and welfare of 'the weak and defenceless person, including the unborn'. However, abortion is acceptable if the life of the mother is endangered or if she could suffer 'irreversible physical injury' giving birth. It also accepts abortion in the case of rape or incest victims. As for artificial insemination, the Army in 1990 found it acceptable only when the donor is the husband; it also expressed opposition to surrogate motherhood.

A number of positional statements were released in 1992. Not surprisingly, the Army came out against gambling as 'detrimental to the spiritual and moral well-being of those who participate'. Gambling, being motivated by selfishness, 'runs counter to the Christian expression of love, respect, and concern for others'. Also it reiterated its opposition to the misuse of drugs, including alcohol, and advocated total abstinence. Consequently 'it actively supports legislation likely to reduce the consumption of alcohol'. The Army expressed its respect for conscientious objectors: 'In no circumstances does the Army regard a Conscientious Objector with any sense of stigma.' Like the Church of England, in the 1990s the Salvation Army has been wrestling with the issue of homosexuality, especially within its own ranks. It issued the following positional statement: 'Scripture opposes homosexual practices by direct comment ... and also by clearly implied disapproval ... Same sex relationships which are genitally expressed are unacceptable according to the teaching of scripture.' However, 'the Army is opposed to the victimization of persons on the grounds of sexual orientation ... Whilst we are not responsible for what we are, we are accountable for what we do; and homosexual conduct, like heterosexual conduct, is controllable ... Such practices, if unrenounced, render a person ineligible for Salvation Army soldiership, in the same way that unrenounced heterosexual misconduct is a bar to soldiership.'

The Salvation Army also believes it has a mandate to contribute to political debate, but here there is far less agreement, either about the kinds of issues on which the Army should voice an opinion or about the nature of the view expressed on moral and ethical

Spreading the news

First published in 1879, the Army's crusading newspaper, *The War Cry*, was sold by its soldiers at meetings, concerts and in public houses. *The War Cry* not only reports Salvation Army news but highlights contemporary issues from a Christian angle.

concerns, as their 'positional statements' make clear. The Army's most senior figure in Britain, Commissioner John Gowans, confirms that the organization is sometimes consulted by governments about specific issues, 'We're considered one of the larger social agencies, so they're quite interested in our view, even if they don't always accept it,' and it has questioned the ease with which credit cards can be obtained, since this can encourage the poor to plummet into debt.

The commissioner insists, however, that 'We don't see ourselves as a politically aligned organization, so there are areas where we think it's not suitable for us to interfere. Where there's a moral element we may say something and as the Salvation Army we're expected to say something. Our position on the lottery is a bit peculiar. We don't take money from lotteries, for example. Yet in some other territories the Salvation Army does. It's true the Army as a whole is opposed to gambling, but William Booth wasn't picky about where he got his money. He would take money from the devil himself. He said so. Because his view was, "I'm not taking it for me anyway, I'm taking it for the poor souls we're helping."'

Phil Wall, of Mission Team, believes that the Army should not be deterred from involvement in politically sensitive issues: 'I think anybody who says the Bible and politics have nothing to do with each other has obviously never read the Bible. Jesus came to challenge every sphere, every stratum of society. The Salvation Army has become known as one of those organizations that have stood with the marginalized. We do that now, in certain ways, and personally I'd like to see us do it more. That may mean we need to become more involved politically. There are issues of injustice and poverty which must be challenged. If there are economic systems that are unjust, then we should be challenging them, and the same goes for government policies. We must be involved in debate and advocacy. The Salvation Army already is, but it should step up its activities. But you must know what you're talking about. If we are going to tell a minister what approach we feel he ought to be taking on certain issues, then we have to know our facts and have done our homework. Within the Army we need prophets, we need politicians who are skilled at working with the system, and we need pastors to deal with the marginalized. We have a lot of expertise. After the government, we are the largest provider of social services in the country. As national and local governments are putting more and more emphasis on the voluntary sector and withdrawing statutory care provisions, our role will become even more important, and that in turn makes it all the more important for our voice to be heard.

'The Salvation Army has always pushed at the boundaries of the law. Remember the case of W. T. Stead "kidnapping" the child who was going to end up being sold for prostitution. It was, strictly speaking, illegal, but it led to the age of consent being raised from twelve to sixteen. I'd argue that the good done by that change was far more significant than the wrong done by breaking the law in the first place. I think people like environmental protesters campaigning at the risk of their lives against the destruction of ancient woodlands or whatever also comes into that category. It's a fine line, I know, invoking a higher law than the law of the land. Don't get me wrong. I'm no anarchist. After all, I was a cop for eight years!'

The Salvation Army took a strong line against the introduction of the national lottery, arguing not only that it is a form of gambling, but that in effect it is a tax on the poor. Phil Wall comments: 'In common with the Salvation Army leadership I was fiercely opposed to the lottery when it was introduced. My line has softened a bit, I suppose. It comes down to a question of, "Do we feed the hungry or do we just proclaim our high principles?"

'I also think we should be more vocal as a movement about whether cannabis should be legalized. I'm not personally in favour of legalization, but I am aware that there are inconsistencies in the law. If alcohol were introduced tomorrow, it would be banned as a dangerous substance, no question about it. The fact that Salvationists are teetotal gives us a particular strength when it comes to raising such matters, and I think we should. I believe Salvationists should take a holistic view of ethical and moral matters. There's too much dualism in most people's thinking today. This division of public and private, secular and sacred – it isn't that clear-cut. When Jack Straw's son was

In the early 1880s a proud corps gathers together, with the sun-centred flag as a backdrop. The bandsmen range in age from seven to seventy.

The Penzance band comes out in force. Then as now, bands assisted in worship, entertained and provided an effective means of recruitment.

found to be involved with drugs, many people called on the Home Secretary to resign. I was completely against that. I applauded the way he faced the issue. It's precisely the fact that a private matter – his son's involvement in drugs – impinged on his public duties that touched me. I think he will have a better understanding of the issues involved precisely because the line between private and public became blurred. Dualism doesn't reflect reality. The old Salvation Army cry is "Heart to God, hand to man!" – in other words paying attention to spiritual and physical needs. Both have to be met.'

Certainly, at corps level, there is ample scope for intervention in issues of local significance. The Raynes Park corps, where Phil worships, recently campaigned against a poster for a pop group called Prodigy, who recorded a song entitled 'Smack My Bitch Up': 'We

were outraged by this. After all, if the song had been called "Smack The Nigger Up" there would have been a huge row. It seems women are an easy target. Eventually the posters were taken down. I then went to the record company and suggested they contributed some of their profits from the group to a charity for battered women. They said no, as I expected, but we thought it was important that they be challenged. I was also very tempted to spray-paint the posters, having first invited the press and the police to witness it. We might have been charged with criminal damage, but it would have been worth it. Anyhow, we got the posters down without having to resort to that. But it does mean that I, in the right circumstances, would be prepared to break the law to fight against oppression or injustice.'

Radical assertiveness, however, is not something that most conservative, law-abiding Salvationists would find a comfortable course of action. In general the Salvation Army prefers more subtle methods

Bandsmen gather in Preston for a regional congress in 1996.

of getting its evangelical message across, and no means is more beloved, or more intrinsic to Salvationist practice, than music. For a thousand years or more the Christian churches have used music in the act of worship. Not only are masses set to music, but countless anthems, hymns and chorales remain in use throughout the world.

William Booth was conscious of the power of music to move the spirit. In this he was no innovator, and in his meetings he could draw on a repertory of hymns already well established not only in the Anglican Church but in the Methodist tradition too. But Booth liked to go one better. Co-opting Martin Luther's question, 'Why should the devil have all the best tunes?' he took popular music-hall songs by the throat, shook them, and put them back down with a new set of morally improving words. Thus to the tune of 'Champagne Charlie' he set the words 'Bless His Name, He Sets Me Free', while 'Here's To The Good Old Whisky, Drink It Down, Drink It Down' was transformed into the alcohol-free 'Storm The Forts Of Darkness, Bring Them Down, Bring Them Down'.

The use of brass bands was also innovative, although it was not one of Booth's inspirations. In Salisbury, in 1878, the Salvation Army had found itself unpopular, perhaps not surprisingly in this most decorous of English country towns. A sympathetic local family called Fry decided to come to its aid by providing a kind of musical body-guard. Since the Frys were all brass-instrument players, the Salvationists found their songs being accompanied by a sonorous band. It soon became obvious that brass bands had other practical advantages too. It was impossible to carry stringed instruments through the streets – at least, not while playing them – whereas brass instruments could be played as you marched and gave out a more penetrating sound in the open air. Moreover they were already popular within working-class culture: many pits and factories had bands, so there was something familiar and comforting about brass instruments in acts of worship.

In the early 1880s a violinist and self-professed atheist called Richard Slater made an appearance at Regent Hall in Oxford Street, where he was so moved by the testimony of a servant girl that he converted to Christianity. He became an ardent Salvationist and offered his services to the movement. In 1883 William Booth set up the music department of the Salvation Army under Slater's direction, while his own son Herbert was given overall responsibility for developing the musical activities of the Army's soldiers and officers. From its earliest days, the Army's members composed new songs, which the music department helped to disseminate. Back in 1881, Fred Fry of Salisbury had already been asked to write new music to meet the growing needs of corps brass bands.

The music department still exists, and its mission is essentially the same. One of its current directors, Captain Peter Ayling, glories under the title of Music Ministries Officer, and he is formally responsible for 'setting the direction and tone' of the British musicians of the Salvation Army. The department publishes about a hundred new songs each year as well as compact discs of music performed by the Army's leading songsters and bands. Some are settings for male voices, others for female or mixed voices, and there are also new pieces for the bands to play. In addition, there are special songbooks for children. Over a thousand new compositions are received each year from all over the world, and the music editorial section has to sift through them and decide which are worthy of eventual publication or recording. The department organizes music summer camps, an idea which originated in the United States in the 1930s. Not only are they enjoyable holidays for the youngsters involved, they also allow the Army to encourage any glimmerings of musical talent among its youth.

Over the years, of course, the style of music has changed. From the beginning, William Booth had no qualms about using popular music to further his evangelical cause, but the Army is still, perhaps, a little squeamish about employing certain idioms that have emerged with suspect associations. Thus jazz, blues and certain forms of rock music, which have strong links with drink or drug culture, are not acceptable to diehard Salvationists. But the Army continues to be flexible in its approach to music, using whatever medium seems appropriate in specific environments. In Scandinavia, for instance,

guitar groups had been popular for decades before they became associated with rock music. Officers running corps have a great deal of discretion in this respect, and while some traditional corps retain a uniformed brass band, others find that their songs are more appropriately accompanied by rock groups or so-called 'worship bands', which consist of any number of disparate instruments. Corps based in multiracial communities may have a gospel choir as well as other musical groups; others have a youth brass band; yet others encourage individual initiatives from musical youngsters to contribute to the worship in their own way. In June 1998 the *Daily Telegraph* noted with alarm that the Army's four hundred brass bands would be joined by guitars, drums and keyboards, apparently oblivious to the fact that the Army had been using mixed worship bands for many years. Brass bands are still used for open-air meetings, and with considerable success. One Salvationist active in the Winton corps near Bournemouth recalls how, ten years ago, 'I went down to Bournemouth pier, listened to the band and became involved with the Salvation Army, and became a full Salvationist in 1993.'

For Martin Neale music has been the glue that has helped keep him within the Salvation Army. 'We are a very musical family. Both my sisters are very accomplished pianists and vocalists and my father was a fine cornet player in his day. My mother is quite talented musically as well. So from the first few days in the world after I was born, I was listening to music. I think it's also a wonderful medium for meditation, a wonderfully spiritual medium. I think that's one of the strengths of the Salvation Army in that we have a multifaceted ministry. I have to say that many times if it hadn't been for the musical interest that held me, especially in my teens, I would not be in the Salvation Army today. I would never doubt the effectiveness of music in the ministry.'

The core of musical expression in the Salvation Army is the *Songbook*, which was first published in 1883. This represents the accumulated musical wisdom of the Army, incorporating hymns and songs old and new. It is revised every twenty years or so, after a specially convened commission has spent years discussing which

Opposite: A close look at the hat-badge confirms that this exuberant Salvationist is from Russia, one of a growing band of soldiers in the former Soviet Union.

The Salvation Army makes use of theatre as well as music to reinforce and communicate its message.

songs should be retained, which should be excluded, and which should be included for the first time. The same *Songbook* is in use in all of the English-speaking countries, although certain countries, such as the United States, publish supplementary material appropriate to their culture. German Salvationists have their own *Songbook* with local material alongside songs borrowed from the standard *Songbook* and translated into German.

Music is disseminated to the faithful not only through published sheet music and compact discs but through live performances by the Army's leading musical groups, the International Staff Band and the International Staff Songsters. Salvationists with a strong musical bent are invited to audition for these groups, each of which unites some thirty-five performers or vocalists. Both groups operate independently of each other, and both travel widely, within Britain and internationally, performing in concert halls and joining in local worship wherever they happen to find themselves on Sundays. Their role is not only to give pleasure to their audiences, but to set the Army's musical standards and act as a catalyst for musical progress. Those standards are also enhanced by the presence of leading orchestral musicians – such as Philip Smith, a trumpet player with the New York Philhar-monic Orchestra, and Dudley Bright, the first trombonist with the Philharmonia Orchestra in London – who are keen Salvationists and give their services to the movement.

The rousing Salvation Army songs appealed to children, and during wartime spells in bomb shelters certainly helped to pass the time.

The Salvation Army also supports ventures into dramatic as well as musical art. About ten years ago the Marylebone Christian Arts Centre was set up in a former Salvation Army hall in Bell Street, not far from Marble Arch. Two performing arts companies, staffed entirely by volunteers, are based here, and they present plays and musicals regularly, although they do not tour. Not all the productions are overtly evangelical or

THE

WAR CRY

And Official Gazette of The Salvation Army.

[INTERNATIONAL HEADQUARTERS.] [Registered at the General Post Office as a Newspaper.] [101, QUEEN VICTORIA STREET, E.C.

No. 741. LONDON, SATURDAY, OCTOBER 11, 1890. PRICE ONE PENNY.

MRS. BOOTH'S PROMOTION TO GLORY

LETTER FROM THE GENERAL.

HER LAST HOURS.

even religious in theme, although they tend to convey a moral or social message. Senior Salvationists have also made their personal contributions to this aspect of the Army's evangelical mission: the current territorial commander, Commissioner John Gowans, has devised the lyrics for musical settings provided by a former territorial commander, Commissioner John Larsson.

If the Staff Band and Staff Songsters set high standards for the Army as a whole, it is, as we shall see, at grass-roots level that the musical traditions remain at their most vibrant. Here, music is intrinsic to the act of worship, and is also, through open-air meetings, directed at those whose souls the Salvation Army is so keen to save.

This two-pronged approach also applies to the Army's news papers. *The War Cry*, founded in 1879 and claiming today to be 'Britain's Most Popular Religious Weekly', features profiles of figures in the public eye, as well as Bible studies, anecdotal columnists, statements about issues of the day and news about Salvation Army centres and activities. *The Salvationist* is more of an internal news-sheet, listing new soldiers and naming those who have been, in Salvationist parlance, 'promoted to glory'; it also offers coverage of developments within the Army, newsworthy items about specific corps and outposts, interviews with leading Salvationists, as well as columns and letters and other noticeboard items.

In Salvation Army language, its soldiers and officers did not die but were 'promoted to glory'. An issue of *The War Cry* (top) reports on the final hours of the life of Catherine Booth.

3

Becoming an officer

AN IMMENSE BRICK TOWER SOARS ABOVE the ridge-line in the leafy South London suburb of Denmark Hill, and ranged around it are the hefty rectangular buildings that constitute the training college of the Salvation Army. The design is imposing rather than beautiful, and the red-brown brick buildings are saved from austerity by the tree-shaded lawns that separate them. Nowadays only about seventy students, known as cadets, live here, making up the members of the two-year courses that the college offers.

Like everything else about the Salvation Army, the training process is no soft option. There is a great need for new officers, but both the procedures for gaining entry to the college and the regime it offers remain as uncompromising as ever. Officers, like aspiring priests or nuns or monks, must feel a divine calling, which is tested repeatedly until both the applicant and the college authorities are certain that it is strong and genuine. Some feel the calling while relatively young; others may have spent many years as soldiers in the Army before feeling that burning sense of commitment required of potential officers. The youngest cadet at Denmark Hill is twenty-two; the oldest are in their late thirties. It is undoubtedly of benefit to the

Cadets participate in Sunday worship at their local corps before entering the training college later in the year.

The gaunt brick tower of the Salvation Army training college dominates the skyline at Denmark Hill in south London.

Army to have so many mature candidates, individuals with a wealth of experience in such fields as teaching, nursing, engineering, and management.

When a soldier feels those first intimations of wanting to be an officer, the initial step is to discuss the calling with local officers. If the consensus is that he or she is serious and committed, the candidate is interviewed by his or her divisional commander and other officers at divisional level. If that hurdle is successfully cleared, the candidate is invited to an assessment weekend. More interviews take place, and included on the assessment panel is a non-officer Salvationist, whose job is to gauge the extent to which the rank and file would regard the candidate as suitable officer material. There are also vocational and academic assessors on the panel, and a considerable effort is made to ensure that the candidate knows what he or she is taking on. For one thing, officers must renounce many of their material possessions as well as their careers.

Three months later candidates are told whether they have passed the assessment procedures. Some are rejected, others are informed that their application is premature and advised to reapply in, say, a year's time. The lucky ones are told that they are under serious consideration as candidates. But that is far from the end of the matter. The next stage is to complete a correspondence course issued by the training college. All this time they remain in the secular world, continuing with their jobs and family life. Their progress is carefully monitored, and on completion of the course they are given the firm decision about whether or not they have been accepted as cadets.

For a single person wishing to become an officer, the procedure is complex but uncontroversial. For married couples wishing to enter the ministry together, there can be many difficulties. One partner may feel a stronger calling; one may be deemed better suited to officership. Should one partner feel a desperate longing to become an officer while the other is lukewarm about it, the ardent partner may be forced to choose between their vocation and marriage. The college staff is well equipped to talk through these issues with the couple, and help them reach a satisfactory conclusion.

Once enrolled at the college, the Salvationists' lives change radically. Because officers are only paid modest salaries, it is impossible to maintain their mortgages or other major financial commitments. Houses must be sold or let. Since the two-year training course is residential, if they are not from London they must say goodbye to friends and family, and install themselves at the college. Married couples are allotted a small flat so they have a modicum of privacy, but the regime used to be much more severe. Captain Anne Read of Winton recalls that twenty years ago there was virtually no fraternization between the sexes; students were allowed to leave the college in the company of a member of the opposite sex only once a week, and on such occasions uniforms had to be worn. In those days there were over a hundred cadets in each year (indeed, in the 1940s there were as many as four hundred), but nowadays the sharp decline in admissions makes segregation impracticable, and the atmosphere at Denmark Hill is considerably less rigid.

Cadets come from a wide range of backgrounds. Many were nurtured within Salvationist families, but they are not in the majority. Others had a Christian upbringing within other churches, but discovered that only the ideology of the Salvation Army could offer them fulfilment. Although a cadet can be dismissed from the course right up to the eve of graduation, dropping out or dismissal is rare. Twenty-eight cadets entered the college in 1996 and two years later all twenty-eight were commissioned.

No cadet can be said to be typical, but Martin Neale's story is not unusual among the older cadets. A thoughtful man, he was aware of a call to the ministry while still young, but, like so many, he also felt the need to build his career. In the mid-1980s he went to live in South Africa, where he became involved in a local corps of the Salvation Army. He and his wife Brenda had a spacious house and gardens, two cars and a swimming pool; he had a career at managerial level and they had no money problems. Yet it was not enough. 'At the end of all that,' Martin recalls, 'there must be something more, a spiritual facet, a spiritual potentiality, which each one of us has. I know that in times of tribulation, when I have come to the end of my tether in the past, it's not been the car or lovely big house that kept me going, but the knowledge of a spirit within me, working within me, empowering me. To be a Christian does not mean that we are exempt from pain and suffering. The difference is that when the crises come, you have something to hang on to. There have been times when I just didn't want to go on, and, had it not been for the spirit of God, I might not be here today.'

In 1990 he returned to Britain with Brenda, also a committed Christian. Both are Scots, so they settled in Inverness, where Martin developed a successful business repairing musical instruments. A keen musician, he had always been a songster and bandsman and greatly loved that side of the Army's heritage. At Inverness he became the bandmaster at the local corps. Their life was going well up in Scotland, and Martin's business flourished, but again he felt, even more strongly, 'the prompting of the Lord'. 'I remember in late October the Lord spoke to us, and it's just a prompting you can't really express in words. You just know you must do this, you're compelled to respond. Brenda and I sat down one evening and we said, "We've got to go to training college, we must be officers, the Lord wants us in full-time ministry." I don't believe being a Salvationist all these years was the overriding influence in my decision to become an officer. I believe that there was something of a plan which the Lord has had for me throughout my life, which he has been working out in me through all my life experiences and all my working experiences. Many of these experiences have not been pleasant at all, but I can now see with hindsight that these things have been for a purpose.'

He considered a ministry in the Church of Scotland, and was even accepted for a Bachelor of Divinity course at Edinburgh, but eventually he and Brenda agreed that the decision to seek officership in the Salvation Army could be deferred no longer. 'I had great respect for the Church of Scotland but I feel that the Lord was saying to me, "The Salvation Army, it needs you, you have particular gifts which can best be used by the Army, musical gifts, and the chance to minister in many styles." I really felt that the Lord could best use me in ministry in the Army.'

A young cadet worships alongside other members of the Southwark corps.

Despite the current debate about the role of uniforms within the ranks of the Salvation Army, these young soldiers from Woking clearly wear theirs with pride.

The Neales set in motion the procedures that would lead to their arrival at Denmark Hill in 1997. They sold their house and Martin wound up his business. Outside the entrance to their top-floor flat in one of the college buildings a handprinted sign proposes the following near anagram: Martin Neale = Traineeman.

Brenda did not have Martin's Salvationist upbringing, but she has been a committed Christian from the age of sixteen. A few years later she became a regular worshipper at a Salvation Army hall in Edinburgh, becoming a soldier in 1978. Not long after, she met and married Martin. Although they are clearly close to each other, their personalities are different: Martin is quiet-spoken, reflective, trim in build and appearance, slightly nervous in manner. Brenda is more obviously articulate and outgoing, a good communicator.

Arriving at college in their late thirties was clearly a culture shock to both. They had been used to independence and to running their own lives. What they were not used to was intellectual rigour, and they had to struggle with the academic side of their training. Martin felt stretched to the limit, but persevered, sustained by his spiritual calling. They were also not used to having their lives structured by a third party. Here, at Denmark Hill, their teachers and timetables were guiding their daily lives. Neither were they accustomed to living in proximity with others, even people who shared their aspirations, and Brenda admits that without their own flat they might not have lasted the first year. She recalled: 'We had had our own home, and suddenly coming into an environment where your time was dictated was very difficult. Every waking moment is taken up with something to do for the college. It's also very pressurized, there's not even a lot of time just to get together and have a chat or a cup of coffee and a good laugh – though we do try. I've never been so tired in my whole life and I have had reasonably pressurized jobs in the past! It's a tiredness that's not relieved by physical exercise, though I do try and exercise when I can, just get out and go for a walk. But what I find is that I do have great joy, great peace. I know the bottom line is that I'm where I'm meant to be and I'm doing the right thing – but I have to cling to that very very hard, and remember why I'm here and what I'm doing it for, because there are times when I stop and think, this doesn't feel like living. An officer has to be a Jack or Jill of all trades, and you've got to be involved in everything, from administration to cooking lunches for lots of people to counselling people or having to break very bad news to people. You have to be prepared to do just about anything. It's not surprising, really, when you think that Jesus was a servant, giving us an example of how we ought to be.'

The average day at college begins with house duties – domestic chores, such as cleaning or repairs – followed by lectures, tutorials, communal lunch, then more tutorials or study periods. Martin's chores included looking after the bandroom, tidying it, putting away the music. On Sundays the cadets would be dispatched to a corps to participate in the worship there.

Not all the training is academic: much is practical, and embraces the social work activities for which the Army is so well known. Since that work is so varied, it is impossible to do more than skate over the surface, and officers later assigned to hostels or outreach missions will receive further training directly related to this kind of work. Nonetheless the Neales are taught how to cope with bereavement, child abuse, alcoholism and other distressing features of modern British society. Martin finds this kind of training remarkably stressful, but recognizes that it is necessary to equip him for the kind of life he will be leading as an officer. On the other hand, there are many positive aspects of the training process. As he walks up the steps into the main building each day Martin enjoys reflecting with pride on the 'great men and women of God who have walked here in earlier generations'. He values the 'unique fellowship' with the other cadets who have also felt the call to the ministry. He appreciates being instructed and ministered to by some of the Army's most remarkable individuals. His biblical understanding has been greatly deepened, and he enjoys the pastoral aspect of the training. One senses that his greatest delight comes from the way in which the ministry incorporates music, to which he is so attached, into everyday worship.

Spiritual training is important too. Officers are required to preach, and for most cadets the business of speaking to a congregation for the first time can be unnerving. Martin acknowledges that public speaking does not come easily to him, but he accepts it as part of the challenge of officership. When he preaches, a training officer keeps an eye on him from the back of the hall, assessing his message, his confidence, his rapport with the congregation, and all the other factors that make up a good preacher. The officer commented: 'Communication is what it's all about, isn't it? I'll look at whether he makes it interesting, whether he captures our imagination, maybe with a bit of humour. I'll look at the songs he uses, whether they follow through the theme he is pursuing. And his eye contact, his voice projection, his deportment. Sometimes the preacher's structure isn't good, the headings don't link up. Sometimes they speak for too long, or it's too short. You need illustration, something to give the address light and shade. Preaching is vital because how are people going to hear about the word of God if it's not preached?'

Whatever success Martin enjoys in this part of the ministry he attributes to the Lord. 'The Holy Spirit was present today,' he declared, after a successful sermon. 'I was thrilled and encouraged by the response of those who wanted to show their love of Christ. The Lord honours those who give themselves over to him.'

For Brenda, prayer is all important. She relies on it to assist her with the preparation of her sermons, and when she preaches she feels that God is working through her. 'I make every step of sermon preparation a matter of prayer because I have to be able to offer people something valuable, something that's going to sustain them, something that's going to encourage them, challenge them, something that's going to keep them going through the week.' Everything of value stems, she says, from her relationship with Jesus, which means everything to her. Without her faith, she might not have survived the various crises in her life.

For Martin too, spirituality is at the heart of the officer's calling. The fundamental quality required of an officer, he affirms, 'is to know the Lord as a personal saviour and to be indwelt by the Holy Spirit'. That the Army is associated primarily with collecting boxes and marching bands is dispiriting to Martin, who believes that it is, first and foremost, a church, a fellowship of believers. It is his knowledge of the Word of God that compels him to give his life to the service of others. Or, as he puts it, 'God created us to have joy in our lives and to care for our brothers and sisters. Thus the priority is to preach the Word of God and develop an understanding in others of the importance of serving and meeting people's needs. We need more witnesses for Jesus.'

Spirituality, however central, is not enough, though, as far as the taskmasters at Denmark Hill are concerned. To become officers, Martin and Brenda must satisfy their examiners on all counts. From time to time they, like all cadets, will be summoned before a 'review and evaluation council' at which their work and progress are assessed. It can be a gruelling experience, as the training officers are not in the habit of pulling their punches, but Brenda is unperturbed: she knows that even the most severe criticism will be expressed 'in love' with the ultimate purpose of making them more effective as future officers. However, a grilling by the review council is no joking matter, and should a cadet perform badly, he or she will be summoned before Major Marion Drew, the senior training officer, for a reprimand. Cadets never forget that they can be ejected from the college at any time.

The climax of the first year at college is the summer placement. In early May cadets are told where they are to spend the summer. This decision is entirely in the hands of the authorities, and cadets have no way of knowing whether they will find the posting congenial. Some fear that summer placement will be the equivalent of being consigned to outer darkness. For most, the outcome is less terrifying. Martin is sanguine. It will, he thinks, 'be an opportunity for me to let down my spiritual hair a bit' away from the closed society of the training college, and free from the pressures of constant assessment. Indeed, he relishes the opportunity to get out into the wider world and put into practice the training of the past year. Brenda is less certain of her feelings, but is comforted by the thought that wherever they are sent there will be a need for their ministry; moreover, the placement will be a preview of their future life as officers. She is anxious about the experience but, as always, commits her anxieties to God. She is also consoled that, as a woman in the Salvation Army, she can serve as an equal partner to her husband, which is not the case in many other churches.

Brenda and Martin Neale took years to decide that they were ready to become officers, but are now fully committed to their new lives.

'Going out on placement,' Brenda mused, 'getting alongside people, is something I enjoy but I do know that that is costly. I'm having to trust to God that aspect of it, because I do get very involved in other people's pain and I have to learn the ability to love them and care for them, to get involved and step back, so that I can be of better use to all people concerned. I couldn't go out and do this placement at all if I thought that it was just me out there. But it's not me out there, it's Jesus who's going to do it through me and that actually takes the fear out of it.'

On 6 May, the long-awaited envelope arrived at their door. They were being sent to Fife, back to their beloved Scotland for the summer. They were delighted, not just because they find their home-land congenial but because they would not be far from their friends and relatives.

Many find the secrecy behind these announcements irksome and unnecessary. Martin feels that it would be sensible to give cadets more time to prepare for summer placement, especially those being dispatched far from their home base. For second-year cadets, the process is even more dramatic: their postings are announced shortly after they are ordained in late May among the pageantry and crowds of Commissioning Day. They must be prepared to pack and move within a few days. Marion Drew says the secrecy is not as traumatic as it sounds. The cadets' particular needs, such as children's educa-tion, the demands of elderly relatives, medical problems, are always taken into consideration, and there is a degree of consultation. Also, it is only cadets who must move at short notice: officers who are given new postings are allowed about six weeks to make the transition.

No one seeks a commission in the Salvation Army as a means of self-enrichment. All officers, whatever their rank, receive a basic living allowance, which begins at £4,024 and rises to a maximum of £5,489. These are single rates, and married couples receive a joint allowance, as well as an additional allowance for each child. They are also provided with a flat or house and, depending on the work they are required to undertake, a car.

Once commissioned, officers will remain on active duty in the Army until the age of sixty-five, when they customarily retire. Then they are given a house to rent, which belongs to the Army, and a small pension to supplement the equally modest state pension. Many retired officers like to remain active, and continue to participate, at a gentler pace, in the work of a corps or outreach centre.

One officer with twenty years' experience longed for more flexi-bility within the structure of the Salvation Army. She knew of some-one who would be keen to work for a year or two in a hospice to broaden his experience of bereavement, and, more generally, to refresh his skills. This kind of sabbatical is rarely manageable within the Army's structure because all officers are required to remain in continuous employment until they reach retirement age, which means there is no chance to take time off to gain experience in other fields, which may be related to their mission but not directly connected with the Salvation Army work.

TWO DAYS BEFORE the climactic Commissioning Day, the atmosphere at Denmark Hill is surprisingly relaxed. For the first-year cadets, who have known about their placement for a couple of weeks, there is no pain. Polis, the first-year cadet from Greece, is stretched out in a deckchair enjoying the spring sunshine. Elsewhere on the campus a football game is in progress. But for the second-years, on the brink of ordination and commissioning, the tension is greater. In just two days' time they will be wearing new uniforms, no longer cadets but freshly minted lieutenants, and they will be hearing from the lips of the most senior British officer, Commissioner John Gowans, about their first posting. A few days after that, they will be on their way, and their new careers will have begun.

Commissioning Day is a ceremony of pageantry and music, as well as prayer, and the cadets need to rehearse. Only a handful are wearing the white shirts with epaulettes that are part of the uniform; the overwhelming majority are dressed in T-shirts and shorts. Although many are on the brink of middle age, from a distance they look like a typical bunch of students. If they seem unremarkable, even dowdy, that is part of their strength: they come across as sturdy, honest, trustworthy, with no edge to them. Kelvin, a stocky, bearded South African, was a former insurance man; Simon an engineer. Both looked rock-solid, unflappable, dependable. Two female cadets stood out from the crowd: Birgit from Denmark, a tall, even statuesque, blonde; and Julia, with glossy dark hair cut into a modish bob. Julia was a fidget, a chatterbox, but had an energy and vivaciousness unimpaired by Commissioning Day nerves.

Simon's calling had come late, and he had had no intention of becoming an officer in the Salvation Army. He had married an officer, however, and because of the strict rules of the Army, she had been obliged to resign her commission once she became the wife of

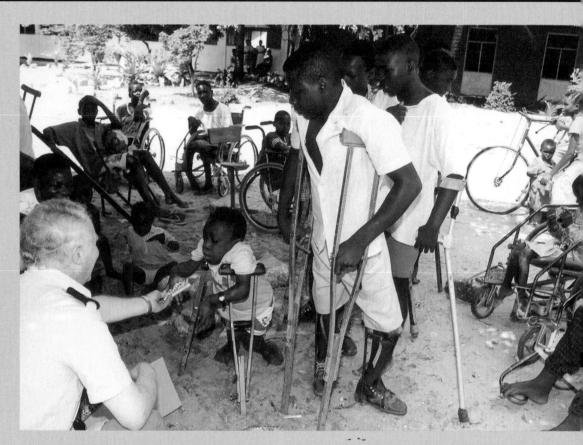

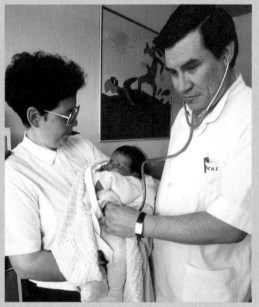

The Salvation Army worldwide

There are few nations in the world, aside from some of the Islamic countries, where the Salvation Army does not preach and reach out.

Above: A Salvationist brings comfort – and sweets – to the children at the Matumaini School for Disabled in Tanzania, which is run by the Salvation Army.

Left: A baby receives expert medical attention at the Salvation Army's hospital in Cochabamba, Bolivia.

Right: A health care project in Quito, Ecuador, ensures that sick children receive expert treatment.

Above and above right: Salvationists in the Caucasus feed the elderly in Tbilisi, Georgia.

Below: If a patient can't make the journey to Quito, the Salvation Army has staff at its health care project to visit rural villages and dispense basic treatments.

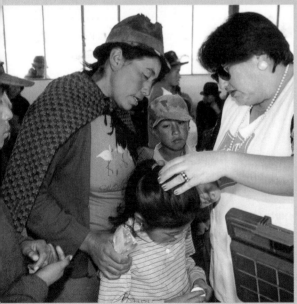

a non-officer. Some six years later, he gradually felt a calling, which resulted in his admission to the training college. Once he is commissioned, his wife, too, will regain the rank she resigned. It seems a cruel choice to impose on someone: the career and spiritual calling you feel so deeply, or the man you wish to marry. Simon intimated that she felt no bitterness since she could still continue her work with the Army even after resigning her commission.

Kelvin's background is more conventional. His family in South Africa were involved in the Salvation Army, so he grew up with it in his blood. It was in 1990, after he moved to Britain, that he felt the call, but it took a few years before he took the plunge and applied to become an officer. He is shortly to be married, and looks forward to a typical Salvation Army officer's career running a corps. For Kelvin, the Salvation Army is a church before it is a social-work outpost.

After rehearsing some of the dramatic routines and songs they will be performing on Commissioning Day, the cadets moved into the assembly hall to practise their sessional song. Throughout the world, cadets undergoing officer training in a specific year are given a sessional name by the General. These second-years were the Builders of the Kingdom; the first-years were the less thrilling Faithful Intercessors. Each session has a song specially written for it, a few of which may eventually be included in the Salvation Army repertoire, but most will be forgotten, except by the cadets who have sung them.

The sessional song of the Builders of the Kingdom was called, appropriately, 'Cornerstone', and leading the rehearsals was Captain Len Ballantine from Canada, who had composed it and was the current conductor of the International Staff Songsters. Like so many Army songs, this was a rousing piece with sophisticated harmonic complexity. For about half an hour the cadets worked on the song until Ballantine was satisfied he had coaxed out of it every nuance.

Captain Ballantine concluded the rehearsal by saying to the assembled cadets: 'Ladies and gentlemen, good luck, God bless you. The next couple of days are going to be exciting, nerve-racking.' One of the cadets presented him with a book and a hug, and they briefly prayed together before dispersing.

When I mentioned to Len Ballantine that I found the idea of a sessional song rather touching, he agreed. 'Absolutely. It gives each year a great sense of identity, knowing that there is this one song that is only performed by them. Singing is such an important part of Salvation Army life, and the tradition of hearty singing blends in perfectly with the fervour of the Army as a movement. Bands, marching, pageantry, songs – these are all part of Salvation Army sub-culture and keep us in touch with the early military-style origins of the church.'

I asked whether tone-deafness would be a serious impediment to any potential officer. 'No,' he replied. 'There is one cadet among the Builders of the Kingdom who is deaf, and she sings just as enthusiastically as everyone else. If she sometimes goes off-key, there are enough other voices around her to make up for it.' This turned out to be the irrepressible Julia, who had indeed been singing lustily during rehearsal while at the same time trying to catch the eye of other cadets on the far side of the hall to whom she wished to communicate some urgent message. Her brother Phil Wall, the head of the Salvation Army's Mission Team, told me that she was able to turn her deafness to her advantage when dealing with people. She has to lip-read, except when she is hitched up to a radio-mike, so stares directly at anyone with whom she wants to communicate. This gives the impression, which may anyway be fully justified, that she is devoting all her attention to you.

BY TWO THIRTY on a warm Friday afternoon, the immense bowl of the Wembley Conference Centre in North London was almost full. Thousands of Salvationists, as well as the family and friends of the cadets down on the platform, were packed into the hall, ready to support the second-years as they took their vows and accepted their commissions. The ordinands were seated towards the back of the platform, flanked on one side by the first-year cadets and on the other by the training officers and other dignitaries, such as Commissioner Gowans and his wife. Gone were the shorts and T-shirts, and all the cadets were clad in their navy blue uniforms, the

Captain Len Ballantine from Canada, composer, conductor and Salvation Army officer, addresses cadets at the training college.

Birgit Jensen from Denmark receives her commission from the Territorial Commander, John Gowans, in May 1998.

women's skirts falling a long way past the knee. Below the platform sat the band, their brass instruments glinting beneath the spotlights.

Most Salvation Army meetings are a blend of songs, prayers, and testimonies, and Commissioning Day is no exception. Three cadets came forward to give their testimonies. A married cadet, Kate Cotterill, spoke, as do others, of her 'ordinariness – except that I belong to the family of God and have a living, vital relationship with God through Jesus Christ'. Brought up by Salvationists, she experienced a childhood that might strike non-Salvationists as bleak: in her own words, no drugs, no rock and roll, no fast cars. In her final year at university she met her future husband and they gradually resolved to become officers: 'You can't evade God's call.'

Julia's testimony revealed that, although the daughter of Salvation Army officers, she was far from ordinary. Brought up in Ulster, she displayed rigid sectarian attitudes as a consequence of peer pressure at school. Arriving in London aged sixteen, she threw herself into a life of parties and endured a disastrous engagement. 'Eventually Jesus came into my life,' she said, and that experience cured her of her rebelliousness. In 1993 she went to Russia to work with street children. 'I had always wanted children,' she confided to the massed ranks of Salvationists in front of her, 'and prayed to God that I would one day have them. Little did I know he would respond by giving me fifty thousand of them.' She had longed to stay on in Russia, working with homeless children, but she had felt the call and had returned to begin her training. Nothing in her speech or manner betrayed that she was profoundly deaf.

Territorial Commander John Gowans then stepped forward to read from scripture and give a short sermon. Commissioner Gowans is a superb orator, and he knows it. He has a lilting Northern tenor voice, which he used to give musical shape to his phrases. He varies his timbre, his speed, his voice rises and falls, moving from staccato declaration to high-pitched fervour. He is not afraid to be tough on his audience, cajoling them, beseeching them, warning them. He is clearly not unwilling to lead from the top, to speak his mind.

In his sermon he noted how Jesus had been a working man, and had often spoken about work. He reminded the audience that becoming an officer had once been known as 'going into the work' and that William Booth had called the ministry 'slave labour for life'. Turning to the cadets, he said, 'You have great gifts and you must put them to use. It's not the Salvation Army that is putting you to work but God who has called you.' They would be well paid for their work, he told them, but not in material things: 'In spiritual values you will be rich indeed, you will never be out of work. The work of God is to make a better world, and you have to work to achieve a better world. But you have to make better people to make a better world! And you make better people by introducing people individually, one by one, to Christ!' It was a message dear to every Salvationist's heart, a reminder that the true work of the Salvationist is the saving of souls.

Then it was time for the cadets to take their vows as ordinands. They affirmed the eleven Articles of War – the Salvation Army's

Julia Wall and Christopher Baldwin present their testimonies to thousands of people on Commissioning Day, May 1998.

credo – and promised to the Territorial Commander that they would abide by them. To each cadet Commissioner Gowans announced: 'I commission you each as an officer of the Salvation Army with the rank of lieutenant.' He then blessed them, and they knelt and prayed. The group had entered the hall as cadets, and left it as lieutenants. A few Salvationists find this part of the proceedings disquieting, as they do not like the notion of ordination, which they claim is a novelty as far as the Army's traditions are concerned. One critic said to me: 'It's been usual in the Salvation Army to see officers simply as those prepared to devote all the time to serving the Lord through the Army. All Salvationists are soldiers of the Lord. Officers are those who serve full-time. Introducing the notion of ordination encourages the tendency to think of the officers as a priesthood, which is contrary to our traditions. There's a feeling that ordination creates a separate class of Salvationists, which troubles a lot of us.'

A COUPLE OF hours later the hall was packed again. The mood had altered, and the atmosphere was boisterous. The band started to play, and the audience clapped as the lieutenants, one by one, or couple by couple, marched in and mounted the steps to the platform as their names were read out. Certain new officers won rousing cheers, according to the size of their clique among the audience, and there was a particularly warm welcome for the foreigners such as Birgit Jensen from Denmark and a Czech couple from Brno, whose supporters had brought an enormous Czech flag with them, which they waved from the balcony. A former general, Eva Burrows, was also in the audience.

Commissioner Gowans took centre stage as the lieutenants marched up; he beamed at them, but did not shake hands. Once they were all in their seats at the back of the platform, everyone applauded them. Then, conducted by Captain Len Ballantine, they sang 'Cornerstone', but the amplification eliminated most of the nuances they had worked on so hard during the rehearsal.

There were more testimonies. Michael Bainbridge admitted that he had not come from a committed Christian background, and until he was twenty-one 'God had hidden himself from me'. His conversion was a gradual process but he has now 'given his life fully over to God'. Birgit Jensen stumbled initially over her words, then tossed aside her notes and spoke, much more fluently, off the cuff. She had come to London as an au pair, and as a joke had attended Regent Hall with some friends. Something about the atmosphere and the expression on worshippers' faces had appealed strongly to her, so she returned to the hall on other occasions. One day she was invited to take Christ into her life. 'And I did.'

Simon, disarmingly, spoke about how he had first encountered the Army when at the age of twenty he found that he fancied a Salvationist girl. Attending a meeting with her he found people who 'had a different dimension' and was attracted by what he saw. It was some years later that he first felt the direct appeal of the Lord – 'Simon, I need you, I love you' – and had come forward during a meeting to kneel at the mercy seat. 'God was changing me, doing a total rebuild of my life.'

The testifying over, the lieutenants staged the morally infused dramatic scenes I had seen them rehearsing, as well as a mime, in which a businessman ignored a homeless person while the soundtrack played Louis Armstrong's 'What a Wonderful World', and some dances to the soundtrack of a gospel song. In the vast spaces of the conference centre, these made little impression. Audience participation was restored as everyone was asked to launch into a rousing song in a happy-clappy vein, 'We Want To See Jesus Lifted High'.

John Gowans then launched into his second sermon of the day, in which he prepared the lieutenants for their new life. He admitted that he had given up, long ago, his right to decide how he would work for the Lord (such decisions are taken, of course, by one's superiors in the military command) in order to gain his true self in the Lord's service. He saw his life as a partnership with Christ in which Christ was the senior partner. 'You just can't say no,' he declaimed, 'to this brilliant, intelligent partner!' He urged those still looking for their true self, or those wishing to renew their commitment to Christ, to come forward and kneel at the mercy seat below the platform, and asked some of the lieutenants to step down and pray with them. The spiritual charge in the air was heightened when he invited everyone to sing 'All That I Am', another splendid Army song with haunting echoes of Sondheim's 'Send In the Clowns'. Sung softly by the thousands seated here, it generated a strange expectancy and stillness in the hall, and gradually about thirty men and women, dispersed around the auditorium, rose from their seats and walked hesitantly down the gangways towards the mercy seat.

There they fell to their knees and were immediately flanked by welcoming officers who flung an arm round their shoulders. One plump young woman fell into Birgit's embrace and the two women talked for about five minutes while the song surged around them. Some of the women were in tears as they finally rose from their prayers and made their way back to their seats.

These intimate spiritual moments were, of course, prolonging the suspense, as everyone keenly awaited the announcements of where the new officers would be sent. Before making those announcements, John Gowans made an appeal for more and better officers, and asked anyone thinking of becoming an officer to join him on the platform. About fifty people rose to their feet and made their way to the front, which must have been heartening, given the recent decline in recruitment. At last, the appointments were made in the manner of Academy Awards: each lieutenant came forward to receive the notification from the hands of the commissioner. An exchange of salutes and it was all over.

When Simon came up to receive his commission he was accompanied by his wife. She had not been on the platform during the afternoon session, but now that her husband was an officer, she had regained her officer status. They were sent to Stoke-on-Trent, Julia to Manchester, Kelvin to Ireland, Birgit to Frederikshavn in Denmark.

To the outside observer Commissioning Day is a curious event. It is an emotional occasion that is milked for all it is worth as the new

officers are welcomed into the ranks, then sent off on their missions for Christ. The audience, or congregation, experiences a growing spiritual charge as the day progresses, the pump regularly primed with songs, music and uplifting prayer. Yet there is something introspective about the ceremony, an inevitable self-satisfaction as the Army enjoys a ritual of renewal as new life is brought into the movement. The word 'cult' has come to have negative connotations, but in the use of its own Salvationist language and jargon, the massed uniforms, the much-loved songs and the succession of testimonies, Commissioning Day comes across to the neutral observer as a closed world in celebration. Few churches reach out to the unloved and marginalized as strongly as the Salvation Army, yet on this festive occasion it looked inward, with pride, with warmth, with a powerful sense of identification and more than a trace of complacency.

The class of 1998 proudly sings 'Cornerstone', the song written specially for them to perform on Commissioning Day.

4

The grass-roots Salvationists

DURING THE HEADY YEARS OF EXPANSION in the 1880s, William Booth and his disciples set up corps as fast as they could throughout the country and, subsequently, throughout the world. That process still continues, with Salvationists struggling to gain a foothold in countries such as Greece and Russia where their presence has never been strong.

However complex and far-reaching the Army's social activities – its hostels and outreach centres, its old people's homes and prison visitation services – its heart remains the local corps. Here the Army manifests itself as a church and not just as a social-service agency. Here it is closest to the surrounding community, offering comfort and care to its worshippers, nurturing the young spiritually and looking after the elderly and sick physically.

There is no such thing as a typical corps. Each officer in charge enjoys a great deal of liberty in organizing and structuring the corps and its activities. Some are traditional, maintaining brass bands and a loyal, if conservative, following. Others go out of their way to appeal to and involve younger worshippers, and offer less traditional, less structured meetings. There is no formula and the absence of liturgy

Visitors from all over the world congregate in Piccadilly Circus – and so the Salvation Army does the same.

and sacraments requires the officers in charge to find means of worship appropriate to the community to which they minister.

Every hall, however modest, is certain to include the various insignia by which the Salvation Army can be identified. A crest will be displayed, bearing the Army's motto 'Blood and Fire', which refers to the blood of Christ and the fire of the Holy Spirit. This was designed in 1879 by Captain William Ebdon. The Army's flag will also be on display: its three colours are red, blue and yellow, which respectively symbolize the blood of Christ, purity and the fire of the Holy Spirit.

For Captains Richard and Valerie Hope, Notting Hill has been their home for the past six years. They have been officers in charge of the church that stands on Portobello Road, alongside the street market, in a district as varied as any in Britain, containing the super-rich, the down-and-out, black hipsters, a generous scattering of prosperous Bohemians and smart restaurateurs, leavened with a sprinkling of pimps and drug-dealers. The church itself is just two doors away from the Saints Tattoo Parlour. When Les Cooper, a jovial volunteer who drives the church's minibus, tries to find a parking spot outside the church, he is usually wedged between a fruit stall and the catering van for a film crew using Portobello Road for a location shot. Les, who is always smartly turned out, contributes a great deal of time to the church, admitting that since he is without a job he likes to keep busy. For Les, helping out at the Portobello Road hall is his way of giving something back to the community. 'If I weren't doing it, I'd be sitting indoors doing nothing, basically.' He is very popular with the pensioners, whom he cajoles and joshes.

Richard Hope is a shy man, which is unusual in the Salvation Army, but his wife Valerie more than makes up for it. A large maternal woman, she is articulate, intelligent, unfailingly cheerful and lacking in self-importance. They spend much of their time working with two categories of needy people: the elderly and the homeless. Valerie sees herself not as a social worker but as someone who is expressing, in the way she knows best, the will of God. 'Everything starts with my Christian belief. I wouldn't be doing all this otherwise. Why would I

Captains Richard and Valerie Hope at the Notting Hill corps, their home for six years.

do what I do, work the hours I do, for next to no money, no stability, no home – why would I do all that when I could have a job and a comfortable life? It's what my Christianity means to me. I wouldn't change what I'm doing for the world.'

Twice a week the Hopes and their volunteers organize meals for old-age pensioners and the homeless, feeding up to 120 people a day. This requires a great deal of preparation, but the procedures are familiar by now and blips are rare. Valerie emphasizes the nutritional value of the meals they provide: 'We use fresh meat and vegetables, and the soups are vegetarian, with a lot of pulses, pearl barley, lentils, that sort of thing. If somebody's got a drug or drink problem, they often can't eat a lot, so you've got to make sure that you get as much good food into them for the little they are eating. There's no point being trendy and giving low-fat diets to the people here, as they need building up. For many of them these are the only decent meals they will get all week, so they need to be nourishing. We charge twenty pence for a meal, which doesn't begin to cover the cost, but it's good

Christmas would be a lonely time for many old people in Deptford were it not for festivities laid on by the Salvation Army.

for those who come here to retain their self-respect by feeling they are not being entirely dependent on charity.'

Valerie accepts that not everyone who attends the lunches for the homeless is necessarily without a place to live. 'We don't ask any questions, you know. Sometimes people think we are being conned, but I don't think anybody gets into a food queue unless there's a need, even if it's a psychiatric need. So we don't ask questions. And I think some people come because they're lonely, or because they're men who have been used to having women around to look after them. Then the woman has died or left them and they don't know where to start, and they come in here a couple of times a week. It doesn't worry me. If there's a need, that's fine.'

She pointed out that she has learnt that you can't always tell who is in need from the clothes they are wearing. 'Some of the people on the street have had private education, some are very well qualified, a lot have university degrees. But various things happen in their life which change everything. Because they're at the bottom, of course, doesn't mean that they'll never get back up. I'm an optimist. We've seen more people sort themselves out, in my time here, than I'd ever have believed. One of our main things is to give people self-esteem. By taking care with the food we give them we are saying, in effect, you are worth something, you are worth the best. I firmly believe that God loves everybody as much as everybody else. We show that God loves people by us loving them. But I'm not a soft touch, really. Doing the best for someone is not always the same as giving that person what they're demanding.

'For some people appearances are extremely important, and if they have a little money they will buy some clothing from a charity shop rather than buy food. Others, of course, will do the opposite. So we do come across people who look well turned out but may not have had a square meal for a few days. You can't tell just by what's outward. It could be that someone has still got decent clothes from better days. You just can't tell.'

Valerie will usually attempt to talk to newcomers at Notting Hill meals, trying to get them to tell their stories so that she can assess how best to help them. But she also knows when to back off. Observing someone who from a distance she perceived as 'very, very disturbed', she reflected: 'He is too uptight. He's obviously been on something, but I should think it's a psychiatric problem. But he looks unapproachable and I wouldn't touch him, wouldn't go near him. You just say "yes" to people like that, because they're very volatile.'

On Sundays the brick hall, which was built in 1924, functions as a church, but the furnishings are sufficiently flexible so that the room, with its baby-blue walls, can be swiftly rearranged to become a day centre and dining room. Most of the pensioners, some of whom Les brings here in his van, are regulars, and before the meal begins Valerie says a few words to them. That day she had a special announcement. After six years at Notting Hill, she and Richard would be leaving shortly and moving to Clapton. She made the announcement in a matter-of-fact way, and it was hard to tell what she was feeling. Some of the elderly people seemed somewhat dismayed, but most know that this is the way of the Salvation Army, that no officer stays put indefinitely, that after a few years everyone must move on in a game resembling musical chairs. No one knew who would be coming to take the Hopes' place. That would only be announced on Commissioning Day.

Valerie seemed resigned to leaving, although she had spent years developing relationships of trust and spiritual closeness with many people in the area. Richard, too, accepted the move without murmur: 'People are much the same everywhere,' he said. 'Still, I'll miss Notting Hill. The Portobello Road is full of characters. I mean, some places I go I look strange in my uniform, but round here I'm just one of the crowd.'

Lunch was served, and the elderly, despite the frailty of some, put away immense helpings of the fresh, wholesome food that the Hopes and their team had prepared. Not surprisingly, these pensioners had nothing but praise for the Salvation Army. 'Bloody good it is here,' said one, in language that may be a touch too secular for Salvationist diehards, 'else we'd starve.' Coming to the day centre, said another, 'is a relief after being in a bedsit with only four walls to look at'.

'Ideally,' said someone else, 'with the welfare state, day centres such as this should be obsolete, but no way are they obsolete. Without this place, many people would fall through the net.' He also praises the way the Hopes make a point of talking to everyone personally. 'They don't have a big salary, and they're only doing it for love.'

After lunch, Mrs Chase came into her own. She is a Salvationist of the old no-nonsense school: upright, tight-lipped, her hair tugged back, and slightly grim in her beneficence. She has become famous for the fact that it is almost impossible to get her to smile. Seated at the piano, she led the pensioners in a round of music-hall songs – 'Swanee River', 'You Great Big Beautiful Doll' – which almost everyone seemed to enjoy immensely. After the songs she led the Lord's Prayer, and Richard Hope read from the Bible. After this brief service Valerie re-emerged to break the news that Mrs Chase had, for the second time, become a grandmother. Acknowledging the happy news, Mrs Chase allowed the thinnest of smiles to stretch her lips. Probably to her alarm, some of the pensioners came up and hugged her. Soon after, Les helped them into the minibus and drove them home.

The Hopes' day was far from over, since the whole operation – minus the music-hall songs – had to be repeated for the homeless. If the elderly are frail, the homeless are somewhat unstable, and a few were already, by mid-afternoon, the worse for wear after indulging in their favourite drug or drink. Despite their volatility, violence is rare. 'If, as very occasionally happens, somebody threatens me,' said Valerie, 'then the other homeless men here immediately become very protective of me. I suppose I'm like a mother figure to some of them. If someone misbehaves, I'll ban them for a week or two, and if it happens again I'll tell them they can't return for two months. But I don't often have to do that. They know that if they want to eat here, they have to obey a few simple rules of behaviour. If you've got any sense, you don't hit your meal ticket over the head!'

At Notting Hill they also hand out clothing, as well as sleeping-bags and blankets, to the homeless. After lunch, when Valerie gave a man a sleeping bag, he seemed amazed to be offered it. After he left, she conceded she had her doubts whether he really was homeless, and suspected that instead he had a psychological problem. 'He may be deceiving me, but I'll go along with it, since he's probably doing no more than looking for a free meal, which he may well need anyway.'

From the wardrobe she produced a few items for a trim man who, she said, was a grandfather, but also a former drug addict. He now helps to sustain himself and his wife by selling the *Big Issue*. 'I remember I once gave his wife a cake when somebody told me it was her birthday, and as she took it she told me that it was the first birthday cake she'd ever had in her life.'

Images of local corps in action: the band at Winton, Bournemouth; Valerie Hope cuddling a child in Notting Hill, and a welcoming officer and Salvationist news vendor at Clapton corps.

On Sunday mornings when the Salvation Army hall becomes a church it typically welcomes some thirty or forty worshippers. Les Cooper stood at the back of the hall, handing out songbooks and Bibles to those arriving. Reflecting the diversity of Notting Hill, the congregation was mixed in terms of race and age. Some of the teenagers wore red T-shirts and form a youth choir. A small music group, led by a guitarist, occupied the side of the platform. A girl stood by a light box on the other side of the platform, so that the words of each song could be flashed on to a screen behind the lectern. Another girl, only thirteen years old, turned out to be an extremely good musician, accompanying herself at the piano as she sang one of her own compositions.

Valerie welcomed the worshippers: 'Our souls are athirst for your giving waters, Lord. Just come, Lord. We welcome you.'

The first song was the popular and rousing 'We Want To See Jesus Lifted High', with its strong rhythms that invite hearty clapping to accompany it. Even the retiring Captain Hope became animated, clapping away and swaying to the music. Mrs Chase was less ecstatic. She had come to church wearing her bonnet, years after it had been replaced by a kind of low bowler. She was not alone, and a couple of other elderly women also wore stiff bonnets, with their flamboyant black bows on the side.

Valerie didn't refer to the order of service but to the 'meeting plan', which had a rather bureaucratic ring, given that it described a relatively unstructured act of worship. After more songs she asked for 'one-sentence prayers' from the congregation after we had had a minute or two 'to sit and contemplate the love of God'. Some worshippers spoke up, thanking God for his love and asking for his blessings. Valerie interjected prayers from time to time, and spoke quietly but fluently, without histrionics. 'We have no embarrassment, Lord, about saying we need you in our lives.'

One Salvationist, Maxine, initiated a question-and-answer session with the teenagers, the moral of which was that while we don't know a great deal about even our best friends, God knows everything about us. Valerie commented: 'It's awesome that God knows everything about us – but it's also comforting.' The teenagers then sang 'Step By Step, On And On' to a backing track, and moved from side to side in accordance with the words, but this performance seemed self-conscious.

Mrs Chase made the announcements, including one about the farewell tea for 'Captain and Mrs Hope', again striking a somewhat formal note for such a poignant occasion.

Then the service loosened up. Mrs Chase's son Peter, a bandsman with the Salvation Army, and his wife presented their new baby, Benjamin, to the congregation, and Valerie offered a prayer for him. Then she asked for 'testimonies' but the worshippers were shy and taciturn, so Maxine rose to her feet to say how the Lord helped her to overcome her fears and anxieties. 'The Lord gives me the grace and helps me, so I don't fall down, I don't stumble.' Victor, a refugee from former Zaïre who had been in Britain for two years, then came forward not to offer his testimony but to sing, in a barely comprehensible French patois, a very loud song, 'Jésu le roi!', followed by another in English, equally opaque, though the refrain was 'More love! More power!'

The sermon was given by Richard Hope, who reflected on their outreach work to the homeless. 'God's grace applies as much to those who haven't succeeded at this stage of their lives,' he said, diplomatically. 'We stand exactly equal before God in the respect that we are all sinners. We all need God's grace in our lives because we are sinners. That's why Christ died for us, because we are sinners.' He spoke about how in their ministry, he and Valerie excluded no one. He had tramped round the pubs selling *The War Cry*, and sometimes conducted funerals for those who died without family or other mourners. Yet he refused to be downcast. 'We tell people no one is excluded from the grace of God, even if they've had a mental breakdown or their lives are in disorder. It's all part of our outreach. We are all God's children, all related, all part of the same family. We're made right by our simple trust in Jesus, who has brought about our salvation. God has done that for me, and wants to do it for every creature on this planet.'

Valerie continued with a succinct prayer: 'Your grace is sufficient for every need in our lives, whether spiritual, emotional, physical.' She brought the service to a conclusion by singing, without accompaniment, a simple hymn, revealing a fine strong voice.

At the farewell tea later in the day Valerie was surprisingly relaxed, considering that she was seeing many familiar faces for the last time. The Salvation Army has a rule that departing officers may not return to their former posts, even for a social visit, for at least a year. This is to give the new officers a chance to establish firm relationships with their new charges, but it seems a bit rough on the leavers.

Over tea, Mrs Chase told me she had lived in Notting Hill since she was five, which made her the senior member of this church by a long way. Forty years ago, she recalled, the hall was much larger, as

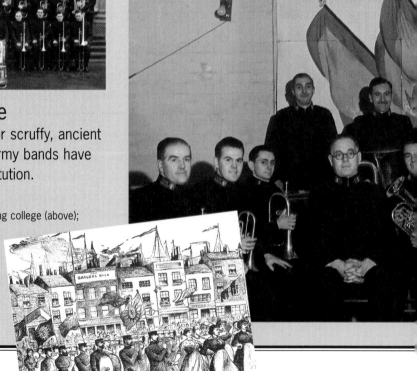

Bands on parade

Large or small, smart or scruffy, ancient or modern, Salvation Army bands have become a national institution.

Bands at the Denmark Hill training college (above); in South Africa in 1920 (top), and in the Salvation Army's heartland, Whitechapel, in 1886 (right).

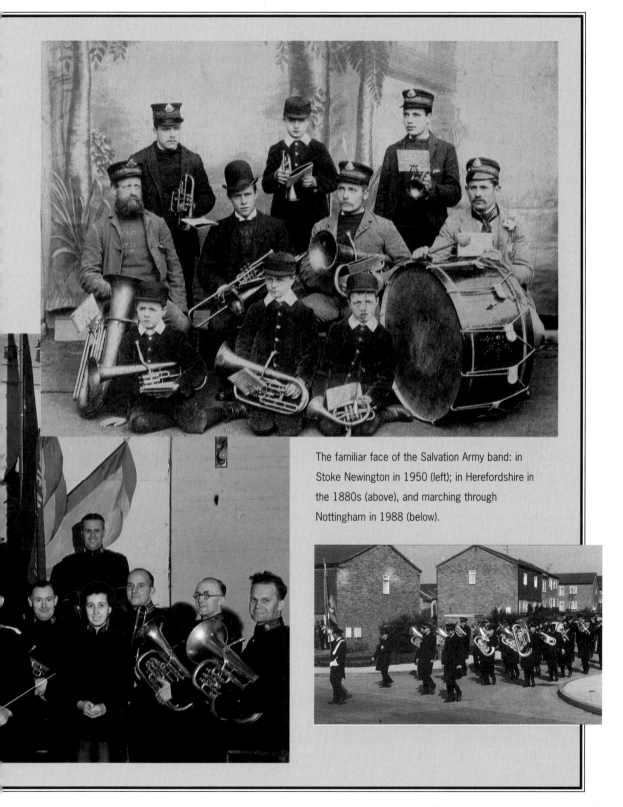

The familiar face of the Salvation Army band: in
Stoke Newington in 1950 (left); in Herefordshire in
the 1880s (above), and marching through
Nottingham in 1988 (below).

the area that nowadays functions as the kitchen was originally part of the church. 'We used to have wonderful open-air services just up near Lancaster Road, at ten, two and six, and then we'd march back here for an indoor meeting. The evening meeting started at six thirty, and if you weren't here by six thirty sharp, you wouldn't get a seat. And that was in the days when we could get three hundred people into the hall, and did. But we haven't had a band for five years or so. A lot of the younger people move away from here or leave. We also don't have the youth movements like the Cubs and Scouts any longer. And parents don't send their children to Sunday school the way they used to. I suppose religion has become less important to many people.' I asked whether the congregation was always racially mixed here. 'Oh, yes, we never turn anyone away,' she said, apparently shocked by the question.

'I've always worked for the Army,' she said, with pride. 'I've never known anything else. My parents were here in the Salvation Army, and my sister was brought up here as well. You have opportunities of serving people in ways that you wouldn't in a church. I mean, all the open-airs and pubs and everything like that. You get to know the people, see them outside, and they get to know you and you make some good friends. I've sung in the pubs, sung "The Old Rugged Cross" many, many a time.'

She accepted the imminent departure of the Hopes as part of the Army's natural order. Indeed, she seemed to approve of change, believing it to be good both for the officers and for the communities they serve. There has to be give and take. 'I mean, we may not like some of things that are done by the new officers, but then they can't like everything we do. So it works, doesn't it?'

Once the tea things were cleared away, Valerie brought the meeting to order: 'Hello, you rowdy lot!' She announced a few songs, and Richard again came into his own, bouncing away and clapping his hands, as everyone sang:

God is good, we sing and shout it,
God is good, we celebrate.

God is good, no more we doubt it,
God is good, we know it's true. Hey!

Then Valerie announced when the new officers would be arriving, and added cheerfully: 'One lot out, another lot in.'

Mrs Chase was not going to be upstaged by all this noisy singing, and, having left the hall with a few elderly worshippers, returned with them all wearing round flat-topped caps with the letters SAOS: Salvation Army Over Sixties Club. Seated in a long row, as though in a boat, they sang 'Pull For the Shore', miming rowing actions. Mrs Chase had to hold her cap on and the rest of the crew couldn't read the words from their songbooks while doing the rowing motions, so it was all a bit chaotic, but nobody minded, and there was considerable hilarity.

Victor from Zaïre, with his wife Françoise, came to the front of the hall to present their new baby to be blessed. Valerie suggested Richard tell the story of how Victor and Françoise came to be in England, but he shied away, so she explained how Victor had fled from Zaïre and how his wife had followed a year later. They never had a proper church wedding in Zaïre 'because there were more bullets flying than confetti'. And they never exchanged rings. So they were married again at this hall, with flowers and wedding cake. Then Richard stepped forward to improvise a prayer for the new baby.

Finally, Valerie said the time had come for goodbyes. She thanked everyone for their support 'and for being you'. 'It will be strange to go to people we don't know and a district we don't know, but that's the Salvation Army for you.' She asked everyone to support the new officers. Richard added a few words. Mrs Chase came up to the platform and crisply handed over cards from the corps and the homeless.

Valerie took up a position at the front door, and one by one people came up to shake hands or hug her. It was a very English occasion. She refused to show emotion, although there was a blur in her eyes from time to time. An old man threw his arm around her shoulder and recited a poem for her. An elderly woman came to take her hand, and Valerie tapped her nose, saying, 'Don't misbehave!', though it was hard to imagine anyone less inclined to do so. Gradually Les loaded the elderly on to the minibus and set off again on his rounds. Then the Hopes went to clear up the empty hall for the last time.

ONE OF THE BEST known meeting halls in Britain is along Oxford Street. Regent Hall began life as a roller-skating rink until its conversion into a meeting hall in 1882. Today it can seat a congregation of 550 and offers free lunchtime concerts as well as a gift shop and coffee shop. Regent Hall attracts a congregation from all over London, both because families who have moved out of central London still like to maintain links with the hall, and because Salvationists are keen to keep the ministry going in such a strategic part of the city. Students from some of the colleges located in central London also find it a convenient place to worship. It is one of the more traditional Salvation Army churches and has a well-known band that marches on Sunday afternoons to various spots within a mile or so radius of the hall. The corps has even held outdoor services in Piccadilly, as well as in quieter parts of Marylebone and along Oxford Street.

The entrance in Oxford Street is modest but leads into a bright modern hangar. The band is seated in the front rows, and there are also a few musicians playing the organ, piano and electric guitar seated to the side of the platform. To one side of the auditorium sit the songsters, all wearing dark blue uniforms. Indeed, uniforms, so rarely glimpsed in other halls, are in the majority here, and to the outsider it may appear somewhat intimidating.

I attended the morning service here on the Sunday before a bank holiday, which meant that many of the families who would normally be worshipping were away on visits to relatives or beaches. From my vantage-point in the gallery, I could see that there were some fairly weird characters down below, not to mention the bearded tramp who was the only other occupant of the gallery. He was an industrious tramp, scribbling mysteriously in a notebook. Down in the main body of the hall I spotted another scribbler, who also felt

Regent Hall, close to Oxford Circus in London, looks gleaming but austere when empty, but on Sundays it is crammed with worshippers from London and from the most far-flung countries.

moved to accompany the songs with his mouth-organ, while on the opposite side of the hall a third man grimaced and twirled his fingers in time to the music.

The Corps Sergeant Major, Richard Stock, told me that these men were regulars at the hall and well known to the other worshippers. Despite their eccentric behaviour, they were not disruptive, and there was something heartening about the way they could feel at home in this setting once a week.

This was an interregnum period: the previous officers had departed for a new posting, and the new ones were not yet in place. The service was conducted by Captain Bill Cochrane, who during weekdays acts as the Salvation Army's external-relations officer. He prayed for those officers who had left and those who were yet to arrive. He expressed a clear belief in God's personal intervention, that He would help the officers with the stress and complications of moving. In his sermon, he ventured a mild criticism of the Army for sometimes giving the impression that this was an officers' army and for not entrusting the soldiers and adherents with enough responsibility, especially since the soldiers are in effect the church.

AFTER THE SLIGHT STUFFINESS of Regent Hall, it was refreshing to visit the church at Southwark, which is located just a stone's throw from the mayhem of Elephant and Castle. No band was in evidence, but most of the platform was filled with the equipment of a combo group: electric guitars, bongo drums, and more conventional drum kits, all of which were played by teenage boys. The minister, Captain Steve Calder, spent most of the service sitting among the congregation, only venturing on to the platform to lead prayers or deliver his sermon. There were about forty people in the church, which is an unusually low turnout for Southwark. Captain Calder estimated that sixty to eighty was the norm.

The congregation here, even more than at Notting Hill, is racially diverse, and Calder's wife Sandra, also an officer, is black. They were married before they went to training college, and were commissioned in 1992. Southwark was their first posting, and they have been there ever since. Steve Calder conceded that it is unusual for officers to remain at a corps for this long, but they had always made it clear that they wanted to work with an inner-city community. 'We want to be able to stand alongside people, to discover what God feels for them and intends for them, and discover the plan that God has for their future. We always wanted to live in a mixed-race community, partly because we believe in multi-culturalism, and partly for personal reasons, because we wanted our own kids to grow up with cultural diversity around them. We have deliberately set out to build a multi-cultural church here in Southwark.'

Church hall activities are supplemented by a parent and toddler group, a junior club for those between seven and twelve, and a number of Bible study groups conducted in individual homes. 'I've always wanted to see the church as people, not as a building,' said Calder, 'so we take our activities and ministry right into people's homes.'

There were no fewer than five newly commissioned lieutenants in the congregation and I soon spotted Simon Perkin and his wife, who were visiting Southwark for the first time, indulging in some church tourism between their years at Denmark Hill and their imminent posting to Stoke-on-Trent. Unlike the other new officers in the congregation, Simon was wearing the pips of a captain on his epaulettes. He explained that since his wife, as a former officer, was entitled to re-enter the officer ranks as a captain, he took her rank as well. He admitted that he would just as soon see all officers as simple captains, without grades such as lieutenant and major to complicate the issue. 'After all, the majority of the people we come in contact with see us as captains anyway.'

I also recognized other members of the congregation I had encountered in other contexts: the deputy director of the Army's men's hostel at Edward Alsop Court in Westminster; and Clive, the

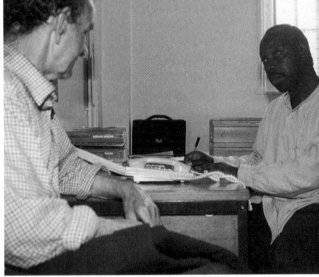

Clive Brown worships at Southwark on Sundays, but during the week he counsels the homeless at the outreach centre on Rochester Row.

The Regent Hall band tunes up as it prepares to parade down Oxford Street on a Sunday morning.

deputy team manager from the outreach centre on Rochester Row. Clive is a regular worshipper here, and his wife Lola, who has an excellent singing voice, leads the gospel chorus and combo band from the electronic keyboard.

Just as Notting Hill had its dour Mrs Chase, so Southwark had its stout, doughty Salvationist soldier, who was on duty at the door, and sat through the service without ever, it seemed, opening her lips. Perhaps she was expressing her disapproval of this new-fangled style of service. It was certainly more charismatic in approach than most others. There were numerous cries of 'Hallelujah!' and 'Thank the Lord!' and during the songs and prayers hands were waved in the air like antennae awaiting a spiritual charge from on high. There were countless small children in the hall – at least three the offspring of the officers in charge – and although at their young age their mastery of the words was less than complete, they were happy to leap up and down to the rhythms of 'Send The Fire' and other popular songs.

Some of the prayers were led by one of the new lieutenants, Jackie, who also sang in the gospel choir conducted by Lola. Her language had charismatic resonances, as she thanked God for giving them the power to overcome the world – 'and that includes Satan in the world'. She denounced those whom she called 'nominal Christians', and said, 'We have to be radical Christians. We need to have powerful, authentic, spirit-filled witness.' One of the congregation's more active teenagers, Darren, easily identified by his Oasis T-shirt, chimed in, asking that Satan be identified in this church before he took root. Perhaps there was a code at work here, but it was far from clear to me what kind of Satanic influence he and Jackie were talking about.

Darren was invited to come up to the platform, where he hoped to demonstrate the properties of fire for the benefit of the children in the congregation. It involved showing how the small flame of a lit match could be easily extinguished, whereas the greater blaze of cardboard set on fire in a saucepan was harder to put out. The moral to be drawn from this exhibition was that the collective flame of Christians was more powerful than single enthusiasm. Unfortunately although the single match was lit without difficulty, the cardboard proved more recalcitrant and it took a while before the demonstration could take place. Captain Calder told me later that he goes out of his way to involve the younger members of the congregation: 'I like to treat them as apprentices, as it's good for them to have an active role in our worship and to participate in our ministry.'

He had no more luck than Darren with his props, a candle, a mirror and a fan heater, which he used during his sermon to illustrate the nature of the Holy Spirit. When the fan heater didn't function (it was intended to illustrate the wind of the Holy Spirit), he decided not to push his luck by trying to light the candle, and continued his sermon unadorned. As he concluded, he invited the congregation to come forward and have their hands anointed with an oil scented with *eau de citron*, which proved a popular idea.

A short time after the service had begun, two men of rather alarming appearance entered and took a pair of seats in the centre of the church. They were hard to distinguish from each other: both had crewcuts, though the elder also had a ponytail for good measure; both were dressed in sleeveless T-shirts which allowed a full display of the many tattoos with which their arms were decorated; both wore blue jeans and black boots. They were attentive to the service but did not participate much, although their boots tapped in time to the music. In one of the seedier pubs in, say, Earl's Court, they would not have attracted much attention, but they stood out like aliens amid the sobriety of a Salvation Army congregation.

After the sermon, when the usual appeal was made for anyone who felt the stirring of the Holy Spirit to come forward and pray, the younger of the crewcut men, Pat, rose to his feet without hesitation and approached the mercy seat. Captain Calder knelt beside him and put an arm round his shoulder. While they prayed together, the choir, directed by Lola, softly sang 'Give God A Try', and the hall's associate minister, a former training-college teacher called Brenda, prayed

The mercy seat

The core of any Army service is the moment when those moved to entrust their cares to God are invited to kneel at the mercy seat, a bench beneath the pulpit, where an officer leads them in private prayer. Even the cartoonist's vision of a rowdy service includes the all-important mercy seat.

for this man who had come forward for the first time. Then Pat rose, embraced Captain Calder and returned to his seat, where his companion shook his hand. As the service drew to a close, members of the congregation came up to Pat and hugged him.

During the after-service care – which attracted a full crowd of children, since it included chocolate ices as well as cups of coffee – there was considerable speculation about Pat, who was seated in the corner, enjoying himself as a focus of attention. One of the gospel singers told me that she had met him at one of the weekly surgeries for the homeless, but had been astonished when she saw him coming forward to the mercy seat. As she spoke of God's wonderful work and love, tears came to her eyes. She told me that although Pat was a relative newcomer to the church, his ponytailed companion, who had been in prison some twenty years ago, was a regular worshipper at Southwark. Pat had been homeless and had spent some time at Edward Alsop Court before being rehoused.

On Sunday morning at Southwark, Captain David Evans preaches to a congregation that listens with enjoyment.

Steve Calder, quite properly, would not divulge the details of his talks and prayers with Pat, but viewed his approach to the mercy seat not as a rush to conversion but as a cry for help. 'I was careful not to force him down a particular road or to exact certain promises from him. Pat is clearly in a vulnerable state, suffering from alcoholism and other medical conditions, and it would have been a mistake to try to lead him in any particular direction. I was more interested in finding out what he wanted and what he hoped that a relationship with God would do for him. I don't believe you can take a vulnerable person like that and force them into some kind of spiritual path or development. Right now the best we can do is give him friendship and fellowship and support, and build on that relationship. He knows he has to deal with his dependency, so there is no point our saying to him: "Right, Pat, you're sorted out with God." It is never that simple. I even worry when I see other members of the congregation rushing

up to welcome him and hug him. Of course they have the best of intentions, but it can be a bit smothering for him, a bit overwhelming. The kind of healing someone like Pat requires is a long-term undertaking, and he's going to need a lot of support.

'The best we can do is offer him acceptance, and help him to find himself. But I am well aware that in dealing with the vulnerable people like Pat we have a high percentage of failure. But it's part of our ministry to try and reach people like that. As far as I am concerned, this matters to me much more than having a band or doing the other things Salvationists are traditionally associated with. There's nothing wrong with a band, of course, but we feel that the important aspect of our inner-city ministry is being alongside people in all their pain and need.'

As I left the hall by a side entrance I bumped into Pat hurrying past and chucking a cigarette into the gutter. He slumped down on the pavement, his back against the wall next to the Salvation Army hall. He looked more like a man in despair than a man whose soul had just been saved, but who could tell what was going through his mind and heart at that moment? It was tempting to speculate that the boldness of his spiritual venture and the warmth with which it had been accepted, not only by the captain but by the whole congregation, had simply left him overwhelmed and confused. Steve Calder was surely right: trying to reach and heal the walking wounded is a long-term project, fraught with difficulty and disappointment.

IF NOTTING HILL and Southwark attracted enthusiastic rather than numerous followers, the same could not be said of Winton, a suburb of Bournemouth, where the Sunday morning meetings routinely drew in over two hundred worshippers, many of whom, however, were not Salvationists but simply regarded the Army hall as their local church. The band here almost resembled an orchestra, and could muster thirty-seven musicians. In the afternoon it marches to various parts of Bournemouth in traditional Salvation Army fashion.

It is hard to say why the Salvation Army centre in Winton is quite so successful. The dynamism of the officers in charge, John and Anne Read, doubtless has much to do with it, but Winton was thriving before the Reads came here in 1996. The community centre opened some ten years ago, and now employs fourteen people, most of them Salvationists, and uses the services of a hundred volunteers. The corps itself is much older: it has been going about a hundred years. 'The managers,' Anne explained, 'work here as part of their commitment to God, which is why they are prepared to accept low salaries.' It seems an extraordinary phenomenon in a nondescript suburb of a seaside town. Bournemouth's large population of elderly people, few of them poor but most living on a restricted income, may account for the popularity of the Winton branch's numerous social services, but not for the enormous size of its regular congregation.

John and Anne have been officers for almost twenty years. They are an attractive couple: John tall and lean with greying hair and a quiet manner, Anne short, pert, with lightly hennaed hair, and decidedly pretty. They spent ten years in northern England and seven attached to the training college in Denmark Hill before being posted here. Their dispatch to Winton came as a surprise, but they are happy here and would be keen to stay on for a few years more.

If there were such a thing as an aristocracy within the Salvation Army, then the Reads would belong to it. John's family traces its attachment to the Army back to the 1870s. His father was a commissioner and, although retired, still conducts Bible study classes at Winton; his mother is also actively involved in the branch. John was not a typical Army child, and remained alienated from it until he reached twenty-four. He trained as a teacher, and worked as a milkman and in various other jobs to sustain his real ambition, which was to be a painter. He also worked as an occupational therapist at a Salvation Army hostel, and gradually returned to the fold when he saw, as Anne put it, 'hope being given to people who were hopeless'.

The most impressive sight at Winton is the enormous charity shop, which fills a disused ice-cream factory that adjoins the church. It is staffed by thirty-two volunteers, one of whom travels at her own expense from as far as Shaftesbury to work there once a week. In the sorting room, cheerful women of all ages rummage through the immense piles of clothing, toys and other gifts. Anything torn, stained, or deemed unsaleable is stuffed into black bags and either sold as rags or sent to the Salvation Army's own recycling centre in Kettering. Diane, one of the shop managers, recalled how one day three hundred items of clothing, mostly dresses and coats, arrived in a single batch, which was piled up to the ceiling.

All day long the shop is busy, as local people, many of them elderly, look through the racks of clothes, the bins of books and records, and the collection of cheap, serviceable furniture. Prices here are considerably lower than at most other charity shops, which surely accounts for its popularity. The stock is also used to supply the local homeless population with free clothing. When the Salvation Army, in conjunction with other Bournemouth churches, organizes meal runs to the homeless, they fling clothes and shoes into the van just in case they run into someone with an urgent need for either.

The Salvation Army flag flies proudly outside the meeting hall at Winton in Bournemouth.

Anne was full of praise for her volunteers: 'We couldn't afford to pay people what they're worth, so we don't try!'

When one of the volunteers was asked why she devotes so much time to the Salvation Army, she replied: 'Don't you think it's worthwhile? All this giving pleasure to people? And there's also a nice crowd working here.' Indeed, the sorting room and the shop were sociable places: many of the volunteers were widows, glad to have a new focus to their lives. Gwen was ninety-two and, although slightly deaf, very much on her feet and proud that many of her grandchildren and twenty-two great-grandchildren have followed her example and are involved with the Salvation Army in Winton. In fact, the middle-aged man I met putting down the carpet in preparation for a wedding due to take place in the church the following Saturday turned out to be one of her grandchildren.

The shop makes a decent profit, since its expenses are so low, and the revenue is used to fund the branch's other activities. These include a daily playgroup held in an enormous room filled with toys and playthings, a mums-and-toddlers session twice a week, and a non-alcoholic bar called the Ark. Identified by a pub sign swinging off a corner of the building, the Ark is intended to give local teenagers somewhere to go in the evening, an alternative to hanging about on street corners or getting drunk in the pubs.

The elderly are given as much attention as the young. Cyril Swansbury, a hairdresser, comes in regularly to give cheap haircuts to pensioners. His parents had been officers in the Army, and he has been in the Winton corps for over thirty years, and played in the band. After he retired ten years ago, Anne told me, 'God opened this ministry for him here.' He also makes home visits, often praying with those he goes to help. In an adjoining room Karen works a few mornings each week, giving pedicures and trimming toe-nails, which are hard for the elderly to reach. There is also a club for stroke victims, offering therapy and other activities.

While many corps, such as Notting Hill, provide meals for the needy, Winton runs a restaurant. It is open all day, but not in the evenings. Prices are low – you can have a complete lunch for £1.50 –

so it is always crowded. Also, like a Viennese café, once a customer is installed with a cup of coffee or a sandwich, there is no pressure to leave. Some of the older people have established their own routines, turning up at roughly the same time every morning, sharing the same table with the same friends, and staying put for as long as they like. A young man at one table told Anne he had plenty of time on his hands to help her out since he had only just come out of prison. Many local Salvation Army supporters come here for lunch, which helps them to stay in touch with church activities. Anne also relishes the fact that it gives her yet another opportunity to help someone out. One of the girls who assists with clearing tables has learning difficulties. Anne explained that as she was regularly occupied here at the restaurant her mother had been freed from the responsibility of caring constantly for her, which had enabled her to adopt a child with Down's syndrome. 'So helping people here,' said Anne with quiet satisfaction, 'can have a wonderful knock-on effect.'

The Salvation Army in Bournemouth has also become involved in local political issues, and to Anne Read this is entirely appropriate, since she feels that the Army has a 'political mandate'. However, in practice it is not always evident what that mandate should be. Three Bournemouth councillors are Salvationists, but that does not mean that they will necessarily promote a point of view in accord with Salvationist doctrine. For example, two of them have supported attempts to legalize prostitution in the town, which, Anne Read insisted, is definitely not Salvation Army policy!

Winton has ambitions too, and its current project is to help establish Salvation Army networks and facilities in the Ukraine. It all started a few years ago when a visiting group from Moscow spoke of the great need in the Ukraine. In 1994 some volunteers from Winton organized a three-week music camp and invited 120 children from Kiev to participate. It proved somewhat chaotic, primarily because of language difficulties. Also, those in Winton were not used to the vicissitudes of Soviet-style culture, and were surprised when some of the musical instruments and other goods that they sent to the Ukraine went missing. 'Our consolation,' explained David Ramsay, a

Salvationist police sergeant deeply involved in the project, 'is that even if something we sent out there was stolen, it still probably ended up in the hands of someone – such as a poorly paid customs officer's child – who appreciated it.'

The Wintonites also found that some of the good work they had achieved at the music camp was not nurtured and developed, since there was no Salvation Army structure in Kiev to build on the foundations they had laid. In time that was put right, and now a local corps is in place. A few Ukrainian Salvation Army officers have been commissioned, although the training period has been shorter than for a British officer. In 1998 the Winton corps sent out three container-loads of practical aid in the form of building equipment. Material selected by the sorters at the branch's shop is also being sent, toys as well as clothes. Nobody at Winton makes light of the fact that the bureaucratic procedures have been nightmarish. Paperwork has been complex, and the Salvationists are constantly aware that the mission may be compromised by documentation problems, red tape and plain old corruption. To help the operation run more smoothly, the Reads organized additional prayers after the Sunday evening service.

In July 1998 six men with practical skills were going from Bournemouth to Kiev and Donesk. There is no point in sending over modern equipment unless somebody is competent to install it, so an experienced builder and a plumber were among the team. One of the projects they hoped to complete was a detoxification unit in Donesk. They also planned to assemble bath/shower units for disabled people in a building adjoining a hospital there. In addition, Winton sent out mattresses, beds, walking frames and twenty-three wheelchairs. Anne said: 'You never see a wheelchair on the streets of Kiev – or a walking frame. And they are very common in the streets of Bournemouth. So you know that anybody who would normally be using one is actually in their home and stuck there. Just giving somebody a wheelchair is really thrilling, because you know that it's going to make the difference between being stuck at home and being able to go out and improve the quality of their life. Such a simple thing, a wheelchair, but it's going to transform somebody's life.'

All six men were paying their own fares to the Ukraine, and had helped to raise the money by organizing sponsored events. For all the problems they have encountered in trying to work in the Ukraine, David Ramsay was convinced it had all been worthwhile. 'For some of the kids who came to the music camp back in 1994, those are the only happy memories they have got.' That experiment will be repeated in 1998, only this time even more children will be involved. At the time of writing, they were expecting some two hundred young musicians to participate.

It must have helped the Reads, and their predecessors, that the Salvation Army allows corps officers so much autonomy. Officers are encouraged to show creativity in their initiatives and are given ample leeway. Anne Read admitted that Winton's sound financial footing helped greatly. As long as no major expense is involved, she and John can make changes or improvements without consulting their immediate superiors at Divisional Headquarters. She gave the impression, though, that the Army's tendency to provide its officers with only short-term appointments was not helpful. Running a branch such as Winton is a complex matter. Not only do so many different activities have to be organized, coordinated, funded and administered, but the size of the operation requires a good knowledge of recent government legislation and such matters as health and safety regulations.

Yet even if the busy Reads might feel that they are running a business rather than a church, Anne insisted that their primary aim remained 'making people Christian': 'The other day we heard that the mother of one of our regular visitors is terminally ill, and naturally the woman was very distressed. As soon as John heard about it, he prayed with her and was able to give her spiritual support. We're always available to people for that kind of help, and there are always people around the centre who are able to pray and listen.'

5

Outreach: the homeless

FROM ITS EARLIEST DAYS THE SALVATION ARMY has gone out into the community to deal with the physical and spiritual needs of the poor and disadvantaged. For many Salvationists, the distinctive character of the Army derives from its fearless inclusiveness. No one is too abject or cast down to be excluded from God's grace. These so-called outreach programmes vary from country to country, according to need. In London and other cities, the Army maintains centres that assist the homeless or those addicted to drugs and alcohol. Where it perceives a need, the Army will try to fill the void. Of course, it rarely works alone, and cooperates with other specialist agencies as well as government-funded initiatives.

No one walking through central London over the past fifteen years or so can have failed to notice the many homeless people huddled in blankets in sheltered doorways. Thanks to schemes such as the Rough Sleepers Initiative, the numbers may be lower than they were a decade ago, but the homeless are still present and still in need. It is estimated that each week fifteen people arrive in London from elsewhere in Britain without anywhere to live or the means to acquire accommodation. These numbers are supplemented by men and

A Salvationist brings soup to a Londoner making the best of dreadful circumstances.

women coming from other European Union countries, often to a job that turns out to have fallen through. Without money, and often without proper documentation, they too end up on the streets. Contrary to myth, they are not entitled to any social-security benefit until they have been in the country for twelve months.

One of the Salvation Army's most visible outreach centres is located on Rochester Row, just off the Vauxhall Bridge Road that leads from Victoria Station to the river Thames. The brick building has been a Salvation Army hall since 1908, but it no longer functions as a church. Its cavernous interior is filled with tables and chairs. In the back are toilets and a shower – a vital facility for those sleeping rough – plus a small kitchen. The centre's principal function is to offer advice. The homeless, contacted by team workers roaming the capital's streets, are given cards with details of Rochester Row's facilities and are encouraged to make an appointment to discuss their circumstances. Back at the hall the team workers are skilled at finding temporary or even permanent accommodation, so long as there are vacancies. One evening a week, Rochester Row functions as a drop-in centre. From seven thirty to ten o'clock the homeless can come here for hot drinks and a sandwich, and can spend the evening chatting, playing cards or Scrabble, or listening to the radio. During the day, when the advice centre is operating, people without appointments will come in and are offered free tea or coffee. The team workers are assisted by volunteers such as Leslie, a retired bookseller from north London.

Apart from the words 'Salvation Army' over the main entrance, there is little inside to suggest that this is an Army facility. The director, Fiona Nelson, is a committed Christian but not a Salvationist; indeed, only two of her team members are Salvationists, one of whom is Stan, an officer from Croydon who retired two years ago, and who comes in every day for a few hours to keep the centre running smoothly and to offer spiritual consolation whenever he feels it appropriate. The Salvation Army pays about half the centre's running costs and works closely with other organizations, such as Equinox, which specializes in assessments for detoxification.

Even in the most chaotic surroundings, Salvationists can befriend and assist those in need.

No one wears a Salvation Army uniform. 'It wouldn't be appropriate here,' said Stan. 'We want a non-threatening atmosphere at the centre, and for some of these men the last time they saw a blue serge uniform was on a prison officer!' Stan sees everybody who passes through the centre – forty-five would be an average day's traffic – and it can be a dispiriting sight, with so many of the men and women being alcoholics, mentally disturbed or seriously depressed. But he is not discouraged: 'No, I'm optimistic. The Lord is very much at work in the world today. I know one alcoholic who was converted to the Christian faith two years ago. Unfortunately he is now back on the bottle, but he has retained his faith, which is pleasing. My own reason for being here is fundamentally spiritual, and my job is to make myself available to anyone who wants to talk.'

The centre aims to treat everyone as an individual. 'We can't solve all their problems,' said Fiona, 'but we can try to work out why they

After counselling at Rochester Row, many clients say hello to Stan in the kitchen. A retired officer, he's the one who hands out tea or coffee.

Below: A Salvation Army poster speaks for itself.

WHO CARES?

have become homeless. The causes could be drug addiction, marital breakdown, loss of a job. Once they have taken to the streets it can be hard to get off them. Quite a few of those sleeping rough are barely literate, which means they don't know how to apply for benefits to which they may be entitled. It's estimated that about one third of those on the streets are without benefits, which means they have to resort to begging or crime. Some of them are useless at budgeting, having no idea what things cost and what they can afford. Others

The outreach centre on Rochester Row near Victoria Station in London.

have no identification, and most hostels won't admit people without ID. We can help with all these things. We'll even put their money into our safe, so they can resist the temptation to spend their savings on drink or drugs when they're trying to save for a down-payment, or for furnishings for a flat that's going to be made available to them.

'One of the problems is that after three months or so on the streets the homeless become accustomed to the life. There has always been a handful of men and women who choose to sleep rough. Those are the people that used to be called tramps. They appreciate some shelter during the cold spells in winter, but in general they seem to be content living on the streets. I know of one man who used to be a chef. His mother died, and as he'd lived with her up until her death, he didn't want to stay on in the house without her. So after the funeral he packed a few belongings and disappeared. He phones his sister once a month to let her know he's okay, and that's it. He comes here very occasionally, usually to exchange an old sleeping bag for a new one.

'He's made a deliberate choice, however strange. But even those who don't choose to be sleeping rough soon find they become part of that sub-culture. Some men have a very organized routine, moving from free meal to free meal, from day centre to evening drop-in. If you plan it right you can eat for nothing all the time, and that means you can spend all your benefit money on drink, if you're addicted. It can become a way of life. And after a while, their appearance will have deteriorated, whatever drink or drugs problem they may have started with will have worsened, and their overall health will be worse too. The longer it goes on, the harder it becomes for them to apply for jobs or hostel accommodation or anything else that will get them out of the rut they're in. What's more, they grow accustomed to the camaraderie of sleeping rough. If we find accommodation for them, they're not always happy, because they are no longer used to being on their own. In other words, they get lonely. In such cases we try to get them on courses of various kinds, where they'll be with other people.

'We define success as any significant change in their way of life. It all depends on their starting point. We have to take things one step at a time. I know of one man who lost his job as the result of a drink problem. Well, he refused to take benefits because he knew he would just spend it all on drink. That made it harder for us to find him

Soup and a sandwich bring a little cheer to this dank corner of Glasgow.

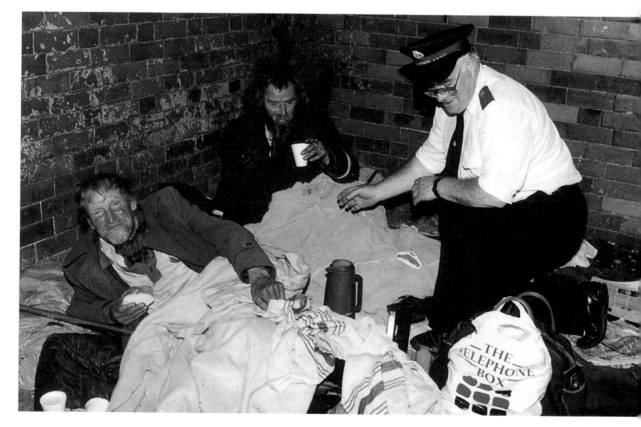

accommodation. Other people are distrustful of hostel accommodation. It certainly used to be a fairly awful experience, with lots of men in dormitories. Some have memories of theft, of violence. Some hostels still admit men with dogs, and turn a blind eye when drugs and drink are consumed. Places like that can be frightening. Others dislike the lack of privacy. On the other hand there are many hostels that are excellent. The Salvation Army's Edward Alsop Court in Westminster is first-rate. Sometimes we'll suggest that someone just goes along there for a meal, so they can see what it's like without feeling any pressure to be admitted. The difficulty is that good accommodation is hard to find, and there are very few vacancies.'

Half an hour before the advice centre was about to open, there were already a few men hanging about outside. Some had spent the previous hours at the Passage, a day centre close to Victoria Station run by the Roman Catholic Church, and were now moving on. As soon as the doors were open, the place filled up quickly, while Stan and Leslie ran relays of cups of coffee to the men outside without appointments. A lean man called Sam managed to get his hands on the centre's guitar. He promised Stan that he would only tune the instrument and not play it, but five minutes later he was playing it and singing along, rather well, offering a medley of Beatles and Eagles numbers. Nobody seemed to mind, so Stan didn't stop him.

Julie began interviewing those who had made appointments for that day. Kevin had come down from Blackpool the night before, and had spent the night at the station. He had been referred here by the Passage as he and his mate wanted sleeping bags. Julie asked if they were interested in accommodation, but as he had no identification with him, his chances were slim. After he left the office, Julie said he had been reluctant to divulge personal details, and she suspected he was simply looking for a handout. If Stan gave him a sleeping bag, it would be clearly marked 'On loan from the Salvation Army', to make sure that he could not sell it then come back for a replacement.

Chris was next. He had been resettled but wanted to get out of his present accommodation. Apparently he had to share the flat with someone who was violent. 'I've had my ribs whacked with a baseball bat, and I'm not staying.' Julie encouraged him to speak to his 'key worker', Doug, who was familiar with his case and would give him advice on what to do next.

'I don't need advice,' said Chris brusquely. 'I'm going to do this my way.'

'But if you just give notice, you'll be making yourself intentionally homeless, and you could make it much more difficult to find new accommodation in the future.'

'I'm probably going over to France in a few weeks, so I don't care.'

'Let me phone Doug. Then speak to him. I'm not telling you what to do, I'm just suggesting you discuss the options before you give in your notice.'

'Phone him if you want, but I'm going to do things my way.'

Julie dialled, and left a message on Doug's pager.

'I'll wait ten minutes for Doug to phone back. If he doesn't, I'm outta here,' said Chris. And with that he left the room and went to a distant table for a cigarette and a chat.

Twenty minutes later he put his head round the door. Doug had not returned the call yet. 'Right, I'm off,' announced Chris.

'You'll talk to Doug before you give notice?'

'Yes.' He was gone, but he had said yes. I told Julie I found Chris a tough customer, aggressive and rather contemptuous of her attempt to protect his interests.

'Yes, but if he'd just wanted to give notice and move out, there was no need for him to come and see me first. The fact that he did so tells me that he's stalling. Which is a good thing.'

Her next appointment was with Sam, who came in with his borrowed guitar and a young Irishman. He wanted to do a deal with Julie. The shower needed repair – some tiles had come off the wall – and, as an experienced handyman, he would do the job for free if the centre would wash his curtains in exchange! Julie couldn't oblige, both because the Salvation Army used its own contractors for repairs, she explained, and because the centre didn't have the facilities for curtain washing. He didn't seem too bothered, and strummed on. He

Hostels and the homeless

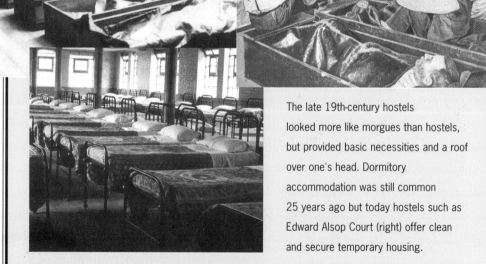

The late 19th-century hostels looked more like morgues than hostels, but provided basic necessities and a roof over one's head. Dormitory accommodation was still common 25 years ago but today hostels such as Edward Alsop Court (right) offer clean and secure temporary housing.

started to talk, rambling, then broke off to touch his forehead and say to me, 'I'm a bit touched, you see.' He offered to play the guitar at the centre's Monday evening Bible study classes, and Julie gave him a songbook so that he could learn some of the favourite Salvation Army songs. He looked dubious, but took it anyway.

'Look, Julie, this is my mate Kevin. He needs a place. Phone round and find him something.' Sam left the office and Kevin sat in his place. With his job-seekers' allowance book and other identification, he at least stood a chance of getting into a hostel that day. Julie started phoning round.

I was surprised at Sam's aggression. 'Yes,' said Julie. 'Sam is probably taking out his frustrations on me by ordering me about, but you have to remember that he has gone out of his way to help out his friend. So he's not just being selfish.' Clive, the deputy team leader, added, 'It is true that many of the people who come here feel that it's their right to have advice and handouts. That's what we're here for.'

EDWARD ALSOP COURT had been mentioned by Fiona Nelson as one of the best hostels in London. It stands on the site of a 1911 Salvation Army hostel in Great Peter Street, a couple of hundred yards from the mother of parliaments. The original buildings were demolished in 1991 and the new one was opened in 1996 by the Queen. It was carefully designed with a view to housing different kinds of homeless people in ways that would be of the greatest benefit to themselves and to others in the building. Like many Salvation Army facilities, it operates under a complex funding system, with contributions from a housing association as well as Army resources. It main focus is the resettlement of the homeless, and it can accommodate 112 men and a few married couples. As well as single rooms, the hostel has some bedsits where men who are about to be resettled can get used to the idea of coping on their own outside an institutional context.

The officer in charge is a Salvation Army major, Margaret Hardy. Her previous assignment was at a women's hostel, and she has had formal training in both social work and management. A few years ago she married another officer and was transferred here; her husband was appointed the officer in charge. Unfortunately he fell seriously ill some months ago, and she had been asked to run the hostel in the interim, which she never expected to do. She is proud of the excellent building and facilities here, and feels that this makes their job easier: 'The newness and quality of the building and the individual rooms have won the respect of the residents. In the old hostel there were men who couldn't be bothered to change their clothes very often or to shave more than once a week. Here we don't need to remind them about these things. We find that if you respect them, not just personally but in terms of the environment you offer them, then you will get their respect in return.'

There are three main categories of resident at Edward Alsop Court: those admitted for a single night; those who are here for a short stay with a view to being resettled in more permanent accommodation; and the long-term residents who are unlikely ever to move elsewhere.

The one-night emergency rooms are on the ground floor. Men in desperate need of overnight accommodation are referred here by other agencies, and sometimes people are brought directly to the hostel, if the need is urgent enough. A one-night emergency case may be admitted subsequently as a short-stay resident.

The first and second floors contain the rooms allotted to short-stay residents. Most of the men occupying them are referred here by various outreach agencies, which may or may not have Salvation Army affiliations. The maximum permitted stay is nine months and after four weeks every case is reviewed. Each 'key worker' deals with fifteen men, exploring resettlement options for them. The workers have an office on each floor of the hostel, so they are easily accessible to the residents. Usually the men are left alone for the first couple of weeks after admission, as they may have suffered some kind of breakdown or trauma and need time to get over it. If they wish, they can be referred to a resettlement programme. The key worker will devise a programme for each man, taking into consideration his skills, budget, family ties and analysis of previous breakdowns. Naturally the key worker is in constant touch with other agencies and with

A joke and a cup of tea at the Ipswich hostel.

Westminster Council's social services department. Some men do not want a structured resettlement programme, just to be installed in a small flat of their own. This, too, can often be arranged, as long as the resident has sufficient means of support. Some are helped to find jobs – one resident drives a bus, for example – or sent on training courses that will give them useful qualifications. A very few end up back on the streets, but that is rare. The basic aim of the counselling and accommodation offered is to break the cycle of homelessness that brought them here in the first place.

Mel was one of the new arrivals at the short-stay unit. He had been born in Britain but had moved as a child with his family to the United States. In New York he had become addicted to heroin, and turned to crime to support his habit. Arrested and taken to court for one of his crimes, he pleaded guilty. This saved him from a prison sentence, but he was deported. Thus he found himself back in Britain, where he had no friends, no family, no means of support. He cannot be readmitted to the United States for five years, so the Salvation Army is helping to resettle him here.

For Mel, a young man of considerable charm, energy and resourcefulness, there was hope. For the long-term residents the future seems to hold a life of quiet decline into old age. There are twenty-nine at Edward Alsop Court, some of whom had been residents of the original hostel that had stood on the site. Many had spent most of their lives in hostels and would have been lost had they been obliged to set up on their own at this stage. 'Some of these men,' explained Margaret Hardy, 'may for some reason, which we don't always know, have stepped out of society, and become anxious about any move that would return them to the ebb and flow of daily life.' The youngest are in their forties, but the majority are in their sixties and seventies. Their cases are reviewed every six months.

Wholesome meals for the elderly being served up at a hall in Belfast.

The rooms are not luxurious, but they are clean, light and airy. On each of the two top floors where the long-term residents live are two lounges, one for smokers, the other for non-smokers. Some residents are involved in jobs like gardening, which get them out of the house during the day; others, who have become institutionalized and are almost afraid to leave this protective environment, are retired. 'It isn't always clear,' said Margaret, 'whether they are truly institutionalized or whether they have simply made a choice to live this kind of life.'

Breakfast and the evening meal are taken in the dining room that occupies part of the courtyard embraced by the wings of the hostel.

No lunches are provided to long-term residents: this is to encourage them to spend their days away from the hostel. Packed lunches, however, are available.

Edward Alsop Court is well designed, impeccably maintained, and offers a standard of accommodation that is surely superior to that available in many university halls of residence. It is tempting to wonder whether its generous level of comfort and care acts as a disincentive to resettlement. 'It depends on their background,' said Margaret. 'We had one man here who, we know from photographs that we have seen, used to play polo in Windsor Park. So he must have come from a very prosperous and privileged background. Then something must have happened, some kind of breakdown that he never disclosed to us. So to that man his simple room must have been quite a comedown after what he had been presumably used to in his youth.

'We had another resident, who died not long ago. He was extremely reclusive and reluctant to talk about his former life. In fact, he never completely unpacked his possessions, even though he was with us for years. He was always very smartly dressed, and if you saw him in the street you couldn't have guessed he was living in a hostel. Well, after his death we had dealings with his sister, and we learnt that he had both German and British royal blood, had been an officer during the Second World War, and had become an architect in civilian life. Then he must have suffered some breakdown that destroyed his life. We don't know what it was. But he lived here because it was the only place where he felt safe. I suspect he may have found himself sleeping on the streets at some point in his life, and that kind of experience can trigger breakdown and mental illness.

'Unfortunately, and inevitably, some of the older men develop senile dementia, but we are not registered as a care home, so after appropriate assessments they may have to be moved to a different institution where they can be properly looked after. The Salvation Army does run some old people's homes to which they can be transferred, while others may be moved to homes run by their local authority. We try to spell out the options and give them as much choice as possible. It wasn't like that in the old days,' she remarked, with a laugh. 'Then they were simply told where they were going and to pack up. They were not consulted. That could never happen now.'

If some of these long-term residents are leading lives of genteel retirement, some of the short-stay men, and a few of the long-term ones too, have more disturbed backgrounds, usually involving drug or alcohol addiction. On admission, each resident signs a licence that spells out the rules they must observe, as well as the standards that the hostel pledges to maintain. The rules include no drugs or bottles on the premises, though there is nothing to prevent residents from going down the street to the local pub. 'It's unfair on the recovering alcoholics to have men drinking on the premises,' Margaret added. 'It's important that they have a "dry" environment.' The hostel managers occasionally check the rooms, which they try to do when the residents are present. Although some of the men are disturbed, violence is rare, but the staff are trained to deal with it should it arise.

The aim of the hostel is resettlement, which is no easy task. It is pretty much a waste of time signing up with the local council, as there is at present a seven-year waiting list for appropriate accommodation in Westminster. Major Hardy and her team work closely with housing associations and other agencies, and clients are encouraged to move to parts of the city or country where there is less pressure on accommodation. But resettlement does not simply involve finding somewhere to live: it usually means finding a job and thus a means of support. 'That's far less easy. We have many young men passing through here who have never worked in their lives, and now lack motivation as well as skills. Others were brought up in residential care until they were eighteen, and aren't used to standing on their own two feet. Many of them have turned to crime rather than honest employment. Some of them are on benefits, which is a help in the short term. But the long-term aim of resettlement is independence, and the benefits system doesn't encourage that. So part of our job is to change the clients' whole way of thinking and to motivate them to change their way of life.'

Although religious conversion is not part of the aim of the management team, they do provide a spiritual context for their work.

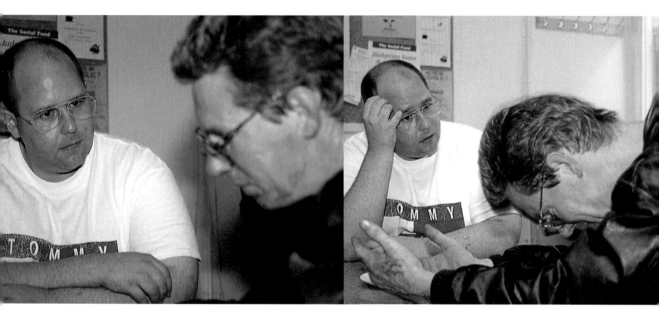

A homeless man, visiting Rochester Row outreach centre, confides in an Army volunteer, himself a former addict.

All the managers, and many of the workers here, are practising Christians, motivated by their religious belief. Their ultimate aim, said Margaret, 'is to point everyone to God'. They meet for prayers every morning and for Sunday worship, but attendance at these is voluntary. Prayers are held in the spacious chapel in the basement of the hostel. Some of the residents requested Bible study sessions once a week and, of course, the Salvation Army was only too happy to oblige.

Major Hardy is not disturbed by the lack of other Salvationists at Edward Alsop Court. 'Our aim is to increase the numbers of the Kingdom, not to expand the Salvation Army.' However, as someone with professional qualifications in management herself, she was not entirely happy with Salvation Army managerial styles, which in her view tend to rely on crisis management rather than on long-term planning. The decline in the body of officers has led to a greater reliance on professionals recruited from outside the Army's own ranks, with consequently a greater likelihood of clashes of management styles. None the less, Margaret Hardy insisted, the Army trains its staff extremely well, and they are all well qualified for the jobs they are asked to do.

IF EDWARD ALSOP COURT shows the Salvation Army at its sparkling best, the hostel for the homeless in Bristol probably offers a more typical example of how the Army copes with a problem that just won't go away. For decades there were two Army hostels in the city, both the old-fashioned kind with dormitories, shared cooking facilities, and unappealing bathrooms. A new hostel was built in the early 1970s, which, it was intended, would replace the two older ones. Typically, some of the long-term residents of one of the older hostels were reluctant to move, so the Army seemed stuck with the costly option of continuing to run two hostels.

The new building is not lovely to look at. A small tower, built of glass and rust-coloured metal cladding, rises above a red-brick structure that houses the offices, lounges and dining room. You will find it just where the M32 motorway debouches into the city. When it was built it offered greatly improved facilities over the older hostels: ninety-six single rooms, and thirty-six more beds in eight dormitories. Still, it was far less advanced in its facilities than Edward Alsop Court. There were no basins in the rooms, which are about half the size of those at the London hostel, although the managers plan to combine some of the rooms to make a few more spacious for long-term residents. Bathrooms are adequate but in need of renovation, which, it is hoped, will also be taken care of in the near future. The managers' task of keeping the facilities in good condition is not eased by the habit of some residents of flooding the bathrooms when they want to air a grievance. From the tower landings you look down on the flat roof below, across which syringes are scattered, a sad reminder that you don't cease to be a heroin addict just because you've been admitted to a Salvation Army hostel. Sometimes prostitutes are encountered in and ejected from the hostel's corridors, and there have been cases when the women, posing as visiting relatives, have abused the residents.

To begin with, the large new hostel was underused. Funded to run at full, or near full, capacity, the managers found that with fewer residents the money did not cover the high running costs. In 1994 the eight dormitories were closed, and the maximum occupancy reduced to ninety-six. Before Bram Tout arrived in 1995 to take over as manager, he had been running a similar hostel in Plymouth. He soon realized that he had to deal urgently with the financial deficit, which needed to be made up out of precious Salvation Army resources. He and his team went out of their way to contact advice centres throughout the city and as a consequence more homeless people were referred to the hostel for accommodation. Contacts with the police, local hospitals and psychiatric hospitals were also strengthened, and this, too, led to increased referrals. Within a short time occupancy at the Bristol hostel had risen to 98 per cent and the centre was financially viable. This was crucial if the facilities were to be properly maintained and essential repairs carried out. Some years ago there were forty long-term residents, but that figure has been halved. 'We aim,' says Bram, 'to have no one staying for more than two years. What we'd like to develop eventually is an old people's unit, where some of the elderly long-term residents can enjoy a better quality of life while still having easy access to the facilities of the hostel.'

Bram also campaigned for access to funding from the Rough Sleepers Initiative, hitherto restricted to London. He achieved his aim: the Salvation Army bid successfully to run outreach and resettlement services under the Initiative in Bristol. Word soon spread through the indigent community that the Salvation Army was now among the leading providers of such a service. 'There has sometimes been a perception that the Army is a bit isolated, that it tends to operate on its own. So some people were reluctant to come to us. We changed all that, and raised our profile. We were attracting so many new clients that the dormitories that were closed down in 1994 had to be reopened. We simply needed the beds. We were also able to take on more staff. When I arrived here there was one project worker and one care assistant for seventy-five residents. We have now recruited four full-time project workers, a shared resettlement officer, a mental-health support worker and even a part-time art therapist. We are also a direct-access hostel, the only one in Bristol, and that means we can offer accommodation twenty-four hours a day, 365 days a year. In the old days we would have shut our doors to new clients at four in the afternoon.' Most of the funding comes from housing benefit, but the Salvation Army pays for all the emergency beds as well as for some of the staff salaries.

The hostel also runs training schemes for its staff, such as 'harm minimization courses', which help them to understand the problems of addiction and to advise sensibly on such matters as the safe use of needles and the avoidance of lethal cocktails of drugs. This is a controversial area, as the Army is not in the business of advising drug addicts on how to select an appropriate vein before injecting hard drugs. The aim, of course, is the long-term one of gradually weaning the addicts off their habit.

'Our participation in the Initiative, which helped us to do all this, also heightened expectations among the clients, who can be quite demanding,' said Bram. 'I was even accused by one client of only doing this job for the money, which is quite amusing when you think of Salvation Army salaries and the fact that I had to sell my house in order to come and work for the Army!'

Bram Tout is a Salvationist but not an officer. He is, in Army parlance, 'lay staff'. His relaxed manner and easy-going humour disguise what is clearly a great strength of Christian commitment. Before they

At the Malvern day centre, a young officer loses the ball and faces defeat.

went to Plymouth he and his wife decided to dedicate their lives to this kind of work. Since the Salvation Army would expect them to rent the staff flats available within the hostels, they could not maintain their previous home, which was sold. Bram's deputy is a Salvation Army officer, Steven Watson, and both men come from Salvation Army backgrounds. However, Bram's wife, although sharing his Christian commitment, is not a Salvationist, which has inhibited him from giving serious thought to becoming an officer. The whole management team at Bristol is Christian, and they take turns in leading prayers and sharing the Gospel with residents. The Christian faith isn't rammed down their throats, however, and Bram has often put residents of other faiths – such as Muslims or Hindus – in touch with local mosques or temples. 'We do have morning prayers in the chapel and special Salvation Army events, but participation is completely voluntary. We can only evangelize to the extent that the residents will let us have that kind of contact with them.'

Despite his Salvationist upbringing, Steven Watson admitted that he knew little about the Army's social-work activities. 'In fact,' he added, 'there are plenty of corps throughout the country that have no idea about the projects taken on by the Army. Even at training college, when I was there a few years ago, a social-work placement during the first year was just one option. Nowadays it's compulsory, so newly commissioned officers have some idea about the work we do and can express an interest in pursuing it once they leave college.'

Both Steven and Bram said that through working at the hostel they had learnt to cope with more or less anything: 'We just never imagined we could do some of the things that we've ended up doing. But God just equips you for whatever task you have to do.' For both men, one of the hardest tasks is ministering a funeral for a resident. 'Sometimes,' said Bram, 'the only people there are Steve and myself. Nothing to mark the past. I come out of there and just weep.'

Once a homeless person arrives at the centre, Bram and his staff establish eligibility and help them to register for benefits, if they have not already done so. The hostel also caters to asylum-seekers, and a number of Croatians and Albanians have passed through its doors over the course of the last year; one or two have been successfully rehoused. Each resident's particular needs are assessed by the staff, who then draw up an action plan. Each resident must pay a 'personal charge', which in 1998 was just under twenty pounds per week, sometimes slightly more depending on the level of benefit received. If a newly admitted person has addiction or psychiatric problems, they may be referred for help to the appropriate agencies. The residents are not obliged to accept treatment for such problems, so long as they do not behave in ways that are disruptive to the other residents. Everyone admitted to the hostel is offered a starter pack, containing soap, toothbrush and toothpaste, shampoo and vouchers for laundry facilities. As at Edward Alsop Court, breakfast and dinner are provided but not lunch.

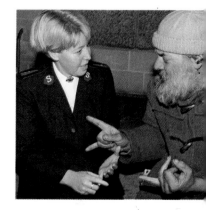

The art of listening: a homeless man in Bath tells his story.

It is rare for the hostel to refuse admission to someone in need of a bed. 'We will do it,' said Bram, 'where there has been a history of violence or arson. We may also refuse admission to someone with a bad debt problem. There is a handful of people who drift from hostel to hostel, running up bills for meals and accommodation, then walking out shortly before payment is due. These people have no interest in resettlement. They simply want to take us for every penny they can get.'

Many residents have severe psychiatric problems. One man in his late sixties is convinced he is forty, that he is a member of the Los Angeles royal family, whatever that may be, and that Bram is trying to kill him. Another, newly released from a psychiatric hospital, was admitted then told to go and have a meal in the dining room while the paperwork was processed. Once in the dining room he slashed his arms with a razor, then swallowed the razor. He was swiftly returned to the hospital. Other residents have threatened to set fire to themselves. One man locked himself in his room and threatened to throw himself out of his third-floor window. Bram had to climb up a ladder and reason with him for thirty minutes before he came down.

There is a high turnover of residents: during the course of the last year almost a thousand men passed through the hostel's doors, and the average weekly turnover is eighteen. The drawback is that few develop any commitment to the hostel and are prepared to contribute anything to running it more successfully. Bram has tried to set up residents' committees, but initial enthusiasm soon dwindles.

'We don't impose a time limit on residence. We have one man who, if you include the years he spent at the old hostel before we closed it, has been here almost thirty-five years! I suppose what we are trying to do is allow each man who comes here to achieve his potential as an individual. There's no single formula. For some it might mean their own small flat and employment; for others it might be supported or shared housing. In some cases the best solution might be a residential home where the quality of life is slightly better than it would be at a hostel such as this. We aim to have most people moved on after about eighteen months, though some men have been here that long and are not yet ready to leave.

'Very occasionally we have to ask someone to leave. If someone is really disruptive, we would try to discuss their behaviour with them. If a man chooses to go to the pub and comes back blind drunk, there's not much we can do about it as long as he doesn't disturb the other residents. But excessive noise, or drinking on the premises, or violent behaviour – well, then we might feel we have no choice but to ask them to leave. Actual violence is surprisingly rare, although with almost a hundred men, most of whom have severe problems, living side by side, there is always a potential for violence. There are small groups of men who give each other mutual support, but I'm surprised how little tolerance there is of anyone's bad behaviour.

'Although we do give men notice and ask them to leave, I am very reluctant to do this. I remember we had an addict called Denis, who kept drinking inside the hostel, and eventually I told him to leave, and I said he couldn't reapply until four weeks had gone by. Well, two weeks later the police found him dead in the streets from an overdose. You can imagine how heart-wrenching it is to receive such news. We can't help asking ourselves whether if we had taken a different decision, Denis might not still be alive. Probably not, but incidents such as that do sometimes make this kind of job hard to bear.'

I asked Bram how he would measure success. 'It varies,' he replied, 'from case to case. Frank has been here for eighteen months and isn't ready to move out, but he is a chronic alcoholic who has not touched a drink since we admitted him. For him that's an enormous success. We have other men who have been here three months but managed to address some issue in their lives. That too can be counted a success. I suppose the ultimate success would be having the place completely empty, but I don't think we'll ever see that day.'

At Edward Alsop Court each floor had its own lounges; here in Bristol there are much larger lounges on the ground floor only. One is spacious enough to accommodate two pool tables and one ping-pong table. Near the pool tables a tall black man with dreadlocks sat quietly, reading, while a young Chinese man contemplated the green baize, cue in hand. Mike, who was a tramp until he was admitted eighteen months ago, sported a handsome white beard. He still likes to drink and to go for long rambles, but his legs are in poor shape, and he can no longer take to the open road for long stretches.

Sitting in a corner of the main lounge was a man who introduced himself as P.J. Munday, a burly man with a forceful personality and a keen sense of humour.

'I've written a poem,' he said. 'D'ya wanna hear it? It's called "Love Is".'

'Go ahead, P.J. Let's hear it.'

'Love is generous,
Love is kind,
Love is always
On my mind.
Love is a feeling
Deep and true.
Love to me
Is people like you.'

I took this to be a tribute to the Salvation Army workers and other people who were trying to help him to stop drinking. He was talking to a young woman who was trying to explain to him the detoxification process she was recommending. P.J. had been there three months and still hadn't succeeded in drying out. His favourite tipple was strong Tuborg – 'Gets the job done quicker.' He laughed.

There is a garden adjoining the hostel, which has been Frank's domain for the past six months. I found him chatting to John in a corner of the garden. John is a large man, moustachioed and impeccably groomed. You wouldn't know to look at him that he is a former alcoholic who had recently endured four cancer operations. He had left the hostel some months ago to be rehoused in his own flat, but a prolonged stay in hospital led to the repossession of the flat and he was back in the hostel. He explained all this without bitterness.

Frank, in his sixties, led me on a tour of the garden he has created. It was a warm afternoon and he had dispensed with his shirt, revealing two words tattooed over each nipple: MILD and BITTER. He had laid out flower-beds and rockeries, and hanging baskets swing from the trees. 'It's all done from stuff that's been thrown away. When they pruned the branches from the trees, I asked them to give them to me, and that's what forms the borders of the flower-beds.' As do recycled skirting boards. Tyres from a local garage have been painted white and encircle shrubs that he has planted. A dessert trolley has been pushed into service as a flower display, and more plants are thriving inside a pair of black kettles. 'The only thing I need badly is more seeds. If anybody reads this and has got seeds to spare, well, we certainly can put them to good use here. Why don't we go to my office for a chat?' he suggested. The office turned out to be a park bench installed on a bank overlooking the rather grubby stream that runs past the hostel. I murmured something uncomplimentary about the polluted water, and Frank reared up. 'What do you mean? There's eels in that stream, and ducks too.' I couldn't tell if he was joking.

For all his robust good humour, Frank has had a terrible life. 'I was abandoned as a baby, and I was kept alive by a dog that came and lay down next to me. It was a cold night, I'm told. So I've always trusted animals more than humans. I've spent most of my life on the streets, wandering from place to place, picking up work here and there. But I was only working so that I could drink. I begged as well. I never had a proper home. I tried detoxification six times, and nearly died twice. But I just couldn't give it up.

'One day I was sleeping in the park near here, and someone coaxed me into the Salvation Army hostel. I didn't want to go, as I thought the hostel was probably an awful place. Anyway, they got me inside, and told me to get warm and dry out – it had been raining that day – and they gave me a meal. They wanted to give me a bed for the night, but I refused. I just wanted to get out of there. The next morning I got my hands on a bottle of wine and a bottle of whisky. I was sitting there, drinking my way through them, and I suddenly thought to myself: Let's call it a day. I went back to the Salvation Army, and I haven't had a drink since. It's been eighteen months. I did it myself. Just stopped. Of course, I've had a lot of support from the people here. I still miss it. Sometimes I get flashbacks, real cravings for drink, the shakes too. So that's why I do the gardening here. It's the only way I can pay them back for what they have done for me.'

6

Outreach:
the desperate

Hate the crime but
counsel the criminal:
Gloucester Prison.

MOST SALVATION ARMY HOSTELS ARE DESIGNED to cater to the homeless, but the women's facility, known as Hopetown, combines a direct-access hostel, a half-way house for those on the path to resettlement, and an 'eventide' home for the elderly. It is in Whitechapel in East London, and provides a direct link with the earliest days of Salvationism. Back in 1875 a woman called Elizabeth Cotterill took a girl into her home to save her from incarceration in an East End brothel, and her goodness of heart is commemorated in the 'minimum support unit' – half-way house – that now bears her name. A few years later, in 1884, Bramwell Booth established a Salvation Army home in Hanbury Street in Whitechapel. In 1931 its facilities were shifted to a renovated school in Hopetown Street. Major Margaret Halbert, now officer in charge at Hopetown, remembers the old hostel as it was thirty years ago, when she was sent there as a young cadet. Somewhat improbably, she recalls it as a happy place, crammed with characters.

The present Hopetown – no longer in Hopetown Street, but in Old Montagu Street, a stone's throw from Whitechapel Road – is a purpose-built structure completed in 1980, when it was opened by the Queen. It was built for the Salvation Army Housing Association, which still takes care of much of the funding, supplemented by the benefits and pensions of the residents.

Other than that it caters only to women, the hostel portion of Hopetown does not differ significantly from the Army's men's hostels. Some clients are referred here by Shelter, the police or outreach workers; others apply personally for admission. Residents pay just under ten pounds a week for bed and breakfast, and can buy additional meals at a modest cost. 'Those women who come here on their own initiative tend to be the most vulnerable,' explained Margaret Halbert. 'They are the ones whose marriage has broken down, or who have had a bust-up with their boyfriend and perhaps been beaten up. On the other hand, the women who are referred here are often addicts or homeless people, and they tend to be more used to this kind of life.'

Hopetown contains fifty-six rooms for the direct-access residents, thirty-five for the elderly, and fourteen for the minimum-support programme. There are ample lounges and kitchens in each wing and on each floor and, as at Edward Alsop Court, the buildings are constructed in an E-shape that flanks a courtyard. Unlike the Westminster hostel, where the courtyard is mostly occupied by the dining room, it is left here as a garden, and indeed one of the more attractive features of Hopetown is the many nooks and crannies where the residents can take themselves for a quiet sit in the sun or to browse through a newspaper. The rooms are larger than those in Bristol, but smaller than those in Westminster; all have basins. Funding from the housing association has made possible all manner of improvements, from new curtains and carpets to renovated kitchens and toilets, which seem in much better condition than those in Bristol. There are no emergency beds, but if it seems advisable to keep someone overnight then a vacant room would be made available or a client can always be made comfortable in the lounge.

Margaret Halbert likes to look on the bright side. One of twelve children raised in Scotland, she worked in a factory from the age of fourteen, before becoming attracted to the Salvation Army and joining the Army's Girl Guide troop. She felt her call at the age of eighteen and entered the training college at twenty-one. From the start she was drawn to social work, and has completed almost thirty years as an officer. 'As a lieutenant I was sent to Glasgow, and there I really saw life in the raw for the first time. Although I had grown up in a large family, I had had a sheltered childhood. I'd never been asked to comb out the beasties in people's hair, for example, or talk to prostitutes!'

Neither her Scots accent nor her Scots resilience has been diluted by years of service throughout Britain. She likes to reflect on the success stories at Hopetown, such as the 'bright lassie' who now has a job and her own flat. She enjoys the way in which many of the staff, even the kitchen workers who are not required to be committed Christians, attend the morning prayers or Sunday meetings. She relishes the multi-culturalism of Hopetown, and is intrigued when some of the Muslim residents prepare feasts to celebrate their own religious festivals.

But she doesn't disguise the failures either. Just a few weeks earlier a girl had checked in for the weekend and had committed suicide two days later. 'We didn't know why. We talk to them when we admit them, but they only tell you as much as they want to, and we tend not to question them too closely at first.' The year before there had been three suicides, and Major Halbert attributes them to drug addiction. Very occasionally there is violence among the residents too. She recalled having to break up a fight at two in the morning between four of the women. One had a knife and stabbed another through the hand. 'But that kind of thing is very rare,' she insisted. 'Many of them arrive here with so much anger, especially if they've had problems with a husband or boyfriend, or a history of abuse. So occasionally that anger gets taken out on the other residents or the staff.'

Life is calmer at the Gardens, as the 'eventide' home is called. Some of the women here are long-term residents who began their stay at the old hostel in Hopetown Street. Florence, the oldest, is ninety-one. The Gardens does not differ greatly from most old people's homes, and has its quota of the sick and demented, but is committed to allowing them to live out their lives in these comforting surroundings. Activities such as the 'reminiscing group' and music and movement classes are popular, but bingo evenings, albeit without the gambling, attract the greatest following. Since the different units at Hopetown are interconnected, the ladies of the Gardens can, if they wish, use the hostel facilities.

Major Halbert's relentless good cheer in the face of every conceivable form of despair can only be explained by her religious faith. 'I love the fact that we are still fulfilling William Booth's mission in the heart of Whitechapel, where he started out. It's love that motivates us here. Speaking for myself, I have always wanted to help people through this kind of work. I still like wearing the Salvation Army uniform. It's so gratifying when people come up to me on the bus and tell me about some beloved Salvationist they knew in their childhood. I find the uniform opens doors, and you'd be surprised how often people come up and tell me their life stories. I find it helps with our witness and ministry. We don't force our Christianity on anyone here at Hopetown, but I'm often asked to say personal prayers for people. It's all part of our ministry, part of sowing seeds.'

WITH SO MANY MEN and women, homeless and otherwise, addicted to drugs and alcohol, it is not surprising that the Salvation Army devotes considerable energies and resources to detoxification units. Greig House, in London's Docklands, looks too fine a building for its purpose, but this is where the Salvation Army dries out alcoholics in London. This handsome red and yellow brick building, with its large white sash windows and perky green clock turret, was formerly a hostel for Scandinavian merchant fleet officers. It sits oddly among the architectural chaos of Docklands, with the Light Railway a few steps away. Its neighbours are artisans' semi-detached brick cottages, and beyond, the towers of Canary Wharf.

Stu Morrison is the director of the unit and, like so many directors of the Salvation Army's social-work operations, he is not a Salvationist but is a committed Christian. He certainly looks the man for the job, a stocky, quiet-spoken, unflappable man in his late fifties

Stu Morrison at Greig House, himself a former alcoholic, combines the roles of counsellor and administrator.

who looks younger than his years. He is unfailingly polite but also seems firm and uncompromising. Not a man, I imagine, that one would want to cross, but on the other hand a man one could trust.

When he counsels those seeking detoxification, he knows what he is talking about. Twenty years ago he was a successful jazz musician, playing all over Europe in some of the most respected venues and frequenting top restaurants wherever he travelled. The dark shadow on his life was that he was an alcoholic. He began to miss jobs and even wrecked a live broadcast by his behaviour. Eventually he was downing methylated spirits and metal polish. 'In fact I still am an alcoholic, but I'm no longer a drunk. One day I found myself hanging on to some railings having just thrown up after drinking some strong lager. Then I saw a beautiful schoolgirl looking at me, at first with fear, then sorrow, then revulsion. I had hit rock bottom and knew it. At that moment I realized it was all over but the dying. If I wanted to rejoin the human race I could, but I was going to have to find the grace and humility to change.' A Salvation Army officer persuaded him to attend a detoxification centre and after three attempts he was off the drink for good.

'When I came to work here I was a care assistant, and gradually worked my way up through the ranks until I became the project manager just over a year ago. Don't expect a lot of fine words from me about what we do here. Our job isn't to deal with the problem but with the symptom. In other words, our basic function is to dry people out. As far as I am concerned, if someone leaves here after ten days without having touched a drink while here, then we have done our job – even if he heads straight for the pub. In fact, we know that most people who have been through centres such as this do return to drinking. This may seem depressing, but it's a fact of life, and I and my team can't afford to be depressed by other people's miseries, nor can we allow ourselves to be frustrated by lapses. If someone does return to the bottle, we'll often readmit him for another drying out. We can do that successfully, but we can't deal with the causes of his alcoholism. One man came through Greig House eleven times, but his liver collapsed shortly before his twelfth admission and he died.

An officer approaches a teenage runaway at a London station.

'What we can do is assess people for further treatment. If the client clearly has specific problems, we may be able to refer him or her to other agencies or organizations that can provide the help we're not equipped to provide. It's not realistic for us to expect that everyone who leaves here is going to become a happy abstainer leading a perfect existence for the rest of their lives. And I've never seen anyone reform their condition to the stage where they can be a social drinker.'

I asked Stu Morrison what a typical day is like for him. 'A typical day,' he replied, 'is when you set out knowing exactly what you want to do, and end up doing none of it. The problem is that we're constantly having to react to things, and that can interfere with the best laid plans. I'm usually at my desk by seven thirty. At nine there's a staff meeting, and at nine thirty we have prayers, then I do interviews

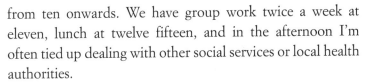

from ten onwards. We have group work twice a week at eleven, lunch at twelve fifteen, and in the afternoon I'm often tied up dealing with other social services or local health authorities.

'The stress comes into it because we are dealing with people who are all at the end of their tether. Almost every day I have somebody sitting across from me on the other side of the desk, saying how he's done wrong – which he hasn't – and let people down and made mistakes. But I don't ever hear anybody saying they have to dash off after our interview because the Ferrari is on a double yellow line and they have to get to a board meeting. The kinds of people who come here are not the controlled drinkers. They are here because they are at the end of their rope. Often they are referred here: by their family, by the local authority, even by the milkman. Sometimes they come in themselves. When we had a detox centre in Whitechapel they tended to come off the street because the drunks were literally on our doorstep.

'There's usually something that triggers off their decision to dry out. Something becomes unacceptable to them or their families, and they are in a state of complete desperation. By this stage, control is not even an option any longer. Although we don't get the controlled drinker here, we do get all classes. We're doing exactly the same as the Betty Ford clinic, the main difference being that we have cheaper carpets.

'Getting off drink is not, as some people say, a question of will-power. It's a matter of choice. You don't need will-power so much as motivation. If you didn't *want* to stop drinking but were a determined character, then you'd need will-power – and you wouldn't succeed. You have to want to stop. Coercion and badgering don't help. I see families bringing in someone, and begging him to stop – ruining his life and health, ruining his family, all the good reasons – but if he doesn't want to stop then he's wasting his time here.

'The old-style woolly-hat wino is almost extinct. We're usually dealing with a more complex phenomenon, as many of the drunks are also misusing prescribed medication as well, and there's a large black market in such drugs. The majority of those who come here are men, though we have the capacity at present to take in four women as well as seven men. We're about to start a rebuilding programme which will result in us having six more rooms.'

Stu glanced out of the window. 'Do you see that? There's a man with a bag climbing up the fire escape. I have a shrewd feeling that he is my first interview of the morning.' He left the office and intercepted the man who, like myself an hour earlier, had failed to find the main entrance to Greig House, which is, in fact, in a building detached from the brick structure.

Stu returned with Charlie in tow. He was tall and solidly built and, as he sat down, I could see that he had a mild case of the shakes, though whether it was caused by lager starvation or nerves it was hard to tell. He insisted, quietly but firmly, to Stu that he wanted to stop drinking, both for his own sake and for his wife's. He estimated that he drank about eight cans of Super Skol strong lager nightly. He began to drink at the age of fifteen, but stress had turned social drinking with his mates into a problem. It was even worse five years ago, when his marriage was breaking up: then he was putting away fifteen cans of strong beer daily, plus a fair amount of vodka. As a consequence he went to a detox unit, but a short time later another relationship took a nose-dive and he resumed drinking.

His drinking apart, Charlie didn't seem to have many problems. Stu asked him a number of questions and urged him to reply honestly, however awkward it might be. Charlie said he had never been in trouble with the police, didn't take drugs, had no psychiatric problems, although he confessed to a suicide attempt about two years ago. 'Don't try it here,' said Stu with a smile, 'or I'll kill you.' An old joke, but it eased the atmosphere, as Charlie was clearly nervous.

Charlie's drinking was not totally out of control. He was, he said, always capable of getting himself home from the pub afterwards and had never experienced memory lapses, although he occasionally had sweats and shakes. He did not work, because of a medical problem that left him prone to sudden blackouts.

The questions over, Stu put down his pen and explained what Charlie was about to let himself in for. 'What we do here is dry you out and get to know you a bit better. I run as relaxed a unit as I can. I'm only as hard as I'm forced to be, which may not be at all. There are a few house rules. No smoking in the bedrooms. If you want to smoke, go down to the lounge and smoke. Smoke in your room, and the alarms go off and we have the fire brigade round in five minutes, and I get fined six hundred pounds. You'll be up at seven and go back to bed at ten thirty at night. For the first week you're grounded, then we assess you and may let you go for a walk after lunch. There are prayers for fifteen minutes each morning and a service on Sunday. You're expected to attend, but you don't have to participate if you don't want to. Just show respect for the organization that's helping you.'

Charlie confirmed once more that he wanted to stop drinking, then signed the admission forms. His wife, he was told, could visit after the first few days. Thirty-six pounds from his benefit payments would go to the centre per week. Stu counted the contents of Charlie's wallet and put it into the safe. Charlie was told he would be medicated with Valium for the first five days, which would suppress the desire to drink. Within about two weeks the physical chain of addiction would have been broken, but the psychological chain might still be in place. He would receive counselling and attend the group sessions, where anything pertinent to a person's recovery would be discussed. These group sessions, in Stu's words, could be something of a bun-fight, as he discourages cosy chat and 'bullshit sessions'. The rest of the residents' time was occupied with household chores, meals, television (only afternoons and evenings), reading and talking among themselves.

The overwhelming majority of residents stay the course, and after they leave are encouraged to stay in touch with Stu. 'I tell them, call me before you reach for that drink, not after you've drunk it. In this job you have to accept that relapses are part of the recovery process.'

As a committed Christian, he is happy to talk about any spiritual anxieties or aspirations his charges may be experiencing. If he detects

Clothing the needy

All over Britain the Salvation Army runs charity shops on high streets, and bargain-priced clothing stores are attached to meeting halls and outreach centres, such as this basement at Rochester Row.

CLOTHES – PRICE LIST
SOCKS - per pair   10p
UNDERCLOTHES/PANTS/BRIEFS 20p
HATS/SCARFS   20p
TIE/BELT   10p
SHIRT   30p
JERSY/CARDIGAN   40p
TROUSERS   50p
SHOES per pair   80p
COATS/JACKET/ANORAK 80p
SUITS   £1.50

more serious religious leanings, which happens but not very often, he will call in a Salvation Army officer. He happily takes a holistic view of the process he is directing. 'As William Booth proposed, we offer soup, soap and salvation – in that order. What we do on the spiritual level was best expressed by one of our clients – rather a rough character, I recall – who said, "I don't know what it is that these people have got, but I want some of it." I do this job because I need to earn a living, but also because I believe it's worth doing. We have the capacity to initiate a complete change in people's lives. Someone once said that we can

open a door to someone who's on Death Row. We show them how to stay alive.'

VISITING IVY NASH was a bit like going to see a favourite aunt. She lives in a modest but spruce terraced house in a well-preserved area of what look like early nineteenth-century dwellings. Faith House is modestly furnished, but full of knick-knacks and personal memorabilia. Ivy is plump and warm-hearted, with a mop of short fair hair, and with a slight shyness that adds to her charm. It is hard to believe that she spends her days working with runaways and prostitutes. Her demure terraced house is in Argyle Street, in the heart of the King's

Cross red-light district. The main living area is on the first floor, as she is converting the ground floor into a room where she can take girls for a cup of tea and a chat. There are also two bedrooms which can, at a pinch, be used to accommodate girls in an emergency, although Ivy insisted that she was not in the business of providing accommodation or meals. During the summer months she is assisted by a cadet on summer placement.

As a child Ivy knew she believed in God, and her best friend came from a Salvation Army background. She became involved with the Army and was not slow to experience a call to greater service, but did not begin training as an officer until she was twenty-six. She is quite convinced that her own calling and skills lie in the area of social work. Indeed, she spent three years in Moscow working with street children, assisted by Julia Wall. On her return she made it clear to her superiors that she didn't want to be given a routine posting. 'I wanted to be stretched.'

While Faith House was being renovated, she spent a year working at Rochester Row outreach centre, but that must have been a piece of cake compared to the challenge awaiting her in King's Cross. 'I knew it would suit me. I already know the language of the street, if you know what I mean. I also knew there would be a lot of violence on these streets, but curiously I never feel afraid. Anyway, it's probably not as dangerous as it used to be, as the police have tried to clean it up by installing cameras, which certainly has deterred some of the kerb-crawlers.'

Most of her work, of course, takes place at night, when Ivy sets off to explore the streets. She is usually out for between two and four hours, depending on the 'traffic'. She is in contact with about seventy prostitutes. She does not wear a uniform – jeans are more usual – but does sport a lapel badge with the Salvation Army shield. She finds it helps to be identifiable, and occasionally overhears people saying, 'She's all right, she's from the Salvation Army.' Uniform, she feels, would be a hindrance. 'I want to encourage people to come up to me and talk, and even to come and worship with us – but most would be put off by the uniform.' She is reluctant to give the girls handouts, although she does provide blankets in winter. If someone comes straight to the door she will offer a hot drink, and perhaps a sandwich. 'But if someone asks for food and I see a can of lager sticking out of a pocket, I'll say no. I can't be seen as a pushover. Instead I can let the people on the streets know that I am part of the community, that I live among them.'

Ivy moves cautiously. 'I don't approach people directly. If I see a girl on the street I'll just smile and walk on. I'll do it a few more times, perhaps for as long as a week, then I might say something like "You all right, then?" To be honest, I don't know what to say to them at first. Eventually they'll talk to me, and we take it from there. Once you get to know the girls, they talk very freely. If a girl is clearly under-age – and the youngest I've come across was only thirteen – then I will go up to them right away and ask if they're all right and if I can do anything to help. If they are on the street because they don't have a place to stay, I can often get them into one of the local hostels, such as Centrepoint.

'The girls will never come off the game unless they have a change of heart and mind. I believe that only God can do this for them. I know there are religious girls out there, and my job is to show the girls God's love, care and compassion. In fact, I don't know a drug addict who doesn't believe in God. Their simple faith amazes me. I won't give up on them. Many of them feel unloved, so they find it hard to understand that God loves them. I tell some girls that I will pray that God will keep them well and happy. It's no use shouting at them or judging them or telling them they'll go to hell, which some evangelists would do. Basically, it's my example that can make a difference: I'm a bridge between the streets and the church. What matters is not what you say to them but what you do. Preaching is not enough. I know that God isn't going to wave a magic wand over these girls. They can experience a change of heart, but they'll still wake up the next morning as drug addicts. The great majority of girls on the game here are into prostitution as a means of supporting their habit. But at least I can let them know that they're not alone and that there are ways out for them.

'I won't give the girls money because I know it will all be spent on drugs. There's one girl I know who needs three hundred pounds a day to feed her habit. So giving her money is hardly going to help her. The best thing I can give these girls is me.'

Not all the girls she encounters and helps are prostitutes. Not long ago she met two runaways and soon realized how vulnerable they were. They had already been approached by a pimp who had offered to find 'work' for them. They had arrived from the provinces and ended up in Holloway before being sent on by social-services officers to, of all places, King's Cross. Once Ivy came across them, she immediately found room for them at a hostel. Girls who are addicted to drugs urgently need detoxification as a first step to getting back on their feet, and here, too, Ivy offers practical help. She does not confine her work to the streets: she accompanies some girls to court, and visits them in prison. She will also try to help the homeless men in the King's Cross area by referring them to Rochester Row, but her main focus is on the women, who are often harder to deal with because they are more suspicious.

Major Ivy Nash, now at Faith House, spent years in Moscow bringing help to homeless children.

Her work is complicated by the transient nature of the street population. She worries when one of the girls she has grown accustomed to seeing vanishes suddenly. There is no way of knowing whether she has moved to another patch somewhere in London, whether she has been arrested, or even whether she is dead.

'It's a very violent world. The violence usually arises when some-one isn't able to pay for their drugs. It can be very frightening out there. There is also sexual violence. One girl, Meg, was picked up and taken back to a room by a man. He had sex with her, then locked her in the room and brought a succession of men back for three days. These were his clients that he was forcing on her. He also rammed a bottle between her legs, jamming it in. When I saw Meg next, her cheek had been slashed down to the mouth. I saw her again recently. She was still drinking but was off the heroin and living rent-free with an old lady she was looking after. There's another girl who came off hard drugs and went on to methadone, but now she's gone back to the needle and back on to the game. She has a pimp, who makes her go out each night and not come back till she's made a hundred and fifty pounds. If she doesn't earn that much, he beats her up. Apart from the awful violence, I can tell that this girl, who wanted to get off the streets and off drugs, is also terribly disappointed with herself. Behind every girl there is a sad tale, some private misery or trauma. Many of them are basically fed up with life.

'I've never been on the receiving end of violence. I don't know why. Some of the dealers and pimps can be very violent people. I suppose my age is on my side. Once I saw a dealer pinning a girl to the wall. She was a tiny thing, just a few stone. So I grabbed his arm and told him he wasn't going to hit her. He was furious with me, said he was going to hit me, but he didn't do anything, and didn't hit her either, as he said he was going to do before I turned up. I didn't feel afraid. I suppose I was used to that kind of thing from my experiences in Russia.

'I would like to stay here a good long time. I think it will be possible for me to stay on – there aren't that many Salvationists who want to do this kind of work! There's often a feeling of evil on these streets. Sometimes I just want to run away. I sometimes feel I can't cope, I'm not used to this world. The verbal abuse is bad and it can get to you. But I do feel I have divine protection.

'I believe with all my heart that the Salvation Army will revive, and that our best years are still to come. I admit we've gone through some bad times, but today we have good leadership. The recent money scandals were very bad for morale. Some good people were reprimanded, because the buck stopped with them. But I feel the Holy Spirit is working in the Army.'

Ivy believes strongly in the work she is doing: 'This kind of thing is what the Salvation Army was doing a century ago, and it saddens me that in some areas the Army has been withdrawing from this kind of work. I feel we are at our best doing quite ordinary things, such as hospital and prison visiting, giving out cups of tea after a disaster, that sort of thing. We also need to be present in the bad areas such as this one. Our presence is most valued not in our meeting halls but on streets such as these.'

ALTHOUGH NOT REALLY an outreach enterprise, the Family Tracing Service performs an equally valuable task, that of bringing long-lost relatives back in contact, which in itself can prove to be a form of reconciliation and healing. Although its name has changed often over the years, it is one of the Army's longest established departments. It was founded officially in 1885, although advertisements in *The War Cry* make it clear that the Salvation Army was searching for, and finding, people from as early as 1882. Throughout the nineteenth century the drift from the countryside and from provincial towns to the capital or the main industrial cities continued. Inevitably, connections were severed, moves were unrecorded, communications were lost, families were broken up. Florence Booth, Bramwell's wife, was entrusted with the task of setting up Mrs Booth's Inquiry Bureau in 1885, and the religious motive behind the enterprise was William Booth's perception that where there was need, emotional as well as physical, people were less receptive to the Gospel. Need and anxiety are barriers to spiritual openness, barriers he wished to tear down.

For much of the present century the bureau was divided into two sections: the inquiry department, which looked for husbands and rogue males who had abandoned wives or children; and the investigations department, which looked for everyone else. When Lieutenant Colonel Colin Fairclough became director of the department, he changed the name to its present one, and the Family Tracing Service employs twenty-three people, most of them full-time. There are no volunteers, since the work involved is usually highly confidential and sensitive. All case workers are committed Christians. Fees are modest and are set at thirty-five pounds, or fifteen pounds for those living solely on a state pension or other benefits, although the average cost of each inquiry is closer to a hundred pounds. The deficit is met from Army resources. In 1997 the service concluded 4,606 inquiries, of which 3,901 were successfully resolved.

Colonel Fairclough has had the typically varied career of a Salvation Army officer. He began as a corps officer in Britain, then served abroad in St Helena, South Africa, the Philippines training college, and Zimbabwe, before returning to Britain. In 1983 he was appointed to the service as a case worker, before becoming its director three years later. Unusually for an Army appointment, he has remained in place ever since, no doubt a recognition that such a job calls for a great deal of experience and continuity as well as skill.

New technology has made the task considerably easier and on an average day ten to twelve cases are solved. Most international telephone directories are now on the Internet. The only problem is that many Internet databanks are expensive to access. The service is fortunate in having been given one of the most useful, GB Accelerator, which normally costs five thousand pounds. With such databanks of names and addresses, it is sometimes possible to locate a missing person in a matter of minutes. But it is not usually so simple, especially in the case of women who have married or remarried and changed their name. It is also tricky to trace people who have left the country. Much of the research still has to be conducted by old-fashioned, laborious ploughing through registers at the Family Records Centre, where the unit maintains two full-time workers. If these approaches fail, then it is also possible to contact organizations – such as trade unions, housing associations, or employers – with which the missing person may have had contact.

Lieutenant-Colonel Colin Fairclough takes satisfaction in having reunited a brother and sister after 81 years of separation.

Occasionally the service declines to take on a case. It will not search for a friend, nor will it pursue adoption inquiries, or search for someone thought to be living in a country such as Saudi Arabia where there is no Salvation Army corps. Colonel Fairclough believes he is the only officer in the whole complex Army bureaucracy who has the right to direct contact with his counterparts in over a hundred countries. It is recognized that, in his line of work, time is often of the essence, and bureaucratic delays need to be minimized.

When the service fails to find the person they are looking for, even though the searcher is disappointed they often write a letter of thanks, praising the team's efforts and sometimes enclosing an additional donation. In Fairclough's experience it is rare that the reaction to failure is anger or bitterness. And even after a missing relative has been located, the story does not always end with reconciliation. Sometimes the relative has no wish to be reunited with the searcher.

Colonel Fairclough recalled a ninety-four-year-old man whose wife had died in childbirth and whose baby son had been taken to live with her family. A short time later he had lost touch with his in-laws and hence with his infant son. In his old age, the father longed to be reunited with his son, and applied for assistance to the Family Tracing Service. Sure enough, they found his son, except that the lad was now sixty-seven years old and had no wish to be reunited with the father he had never known. Similar situations arise with children abandoned by their mother, especially if born out of wedlock, and usually the case worker has no choice but to accept no for an answer. However, if they discern any ambivalence in the response, they may press a bit, which sometimes results in a change of heart.

'We always have to remember,' said Colonel Fairclough, 'that we only ever hear one side of the story. I recall a girl who vanished just after she left university. Her parents came to us and begged us to find her. And we did. When we talked to her, she explained that she had been abused by her parents, who were involved in sado-masochistic practices, and that she had spent much of her university years in counselling, trying to recover from the experience.' She had deliberately severed contact with her parents, and had no wish to see them. Simply being contacted by the service re-ignited the terrors and anxieties she had left behind. Of course, the service made no further effort to bring parents and daughter together.

Sometimes the unit simply gets it wrong. Colonel Fairclough recalled one case in which they had the name of the missing man, the name of his wife, the approximate area in which he was supposed to be living, and his date of birth. A computer search revealed that this man had recently died, and the service informed the client of his demise. A few weeks later, the man turned up, alive and well. It was a case of pure coincidence: two men sharing the same basic data.

As always with the Salvation Army, there is a spiritual agenda to the service offered. Behind the attempt to reunite dispersed relatives lies a ministry, to which those concerned may turn. Colonel Fairclough has received letters saying that not only is a family together again but their faith has been restored. People testify to a wish to 'return to the fold'. The unit is not overtly proselytizing, but they see themselves as more than a detective agency: there is a spiritual motivation. Sometimes when speaking to people on the phone or at the service offices, Fairclough or his staff will pray with them. 'The motivation behind all this is reconciliation and healing, which has a spiritual dimension in a family setting. We also find, on occasion, that there are psychosomatic benefits to reconciliation. I know of cases where people who have been quite ill have made a recovery once they have been reunited with a lost relative.'

Although they appear to be reuniting just two people, they are often bringing together an entire extended family. It is hard to underestimate how the absence of a close relative can leave a void in a person's life, explained Colonel Fairclough. It is not easy to say what, after years or decades of living with that void, triggers the desire to find the missing person. In some cases they have not been aware that they have a sibling, until, perhaps, some other relative lets the cat out of the bag. Intimations of mortality, or the death of another relative, may also prompt a search: one inquiry was made, successfully, after siblings had been separated for eighty-one years. Sometimes a woman about to get married wants her missing parent to be present.

Once in a while the service is stumped. A recent bulletin quoted a letter: 'I was born of white English parents. When I was small, I was injected with a brown liquid which turned me from white to black. My mum and my dad live in a large mansion which is guarded by soldiers.' As the bulletin noted, this 'left us with a few doubts as to how we might proceed'.

7

The man at the top

AS TERRITORIAL COMMANDER FOR GREAT BRITAIN and the Republic of Ireland, Commissioner John Gowans is the most senior figure in the British Salvation Army. He received this final promotion towards the end of his long career, which has seen him serving the Army not just in Britain but in France, Australia and the USA. He sports a goatee beard, and he has retained, despite long spells abroad, his northern accent.

A powerful orator in the public arena, John Gowans is measured without being austere, reflective without being pompous. He does not stand on ceremony, and gives the impression of being selective about those parts of the Salvation Army tradition he finds admirable and those he finds more tiresome. It would be dangerous to try to summarize his theological drive in a single sentence but, from his sermons and public addresses, he believes fervently in the notion of a personal relationship with Christ as the foundation of religious conviction and action.

Commissioner Gowans is thoroughly aware of the immense problems that the Salvation Army is facing. A market-research firm has been commissioned to examine public attitudes to the Army and to

Commissioner John Gowans, Territorial Commander for Great Britain and Ireland.

Communicating through song: Country and Western, a communal singsong and a children's songster group, all at Woking corps.

help it devise strategies for the future. The Army has also established the Vision Action Group, which operates under the chairmanship of the Chief Secretary of the Salvation Army in Britain, Colonel Douglas Davis, but it is unthinkable that any major decisions will be taken without the consent of the Territorial Commander. It seems unfortunate that Gowans has been appointed to his important post just a few years before he must retire from active service: given the profound problems the church is facing, it might perhaps have been wiser to give the man at the top a longer opportunity to tackle the difficulties and turn things round. But it has always been part of the Army's culture to be wary of long-term, entrenched appointments.

John Gowans knows the Salvation Army has a fusty image that is at odds with its engagement in social activities few other churches would touch. 'From the survey that we've commissioned we're amazed to discover that more than half the people in this country understand that the Salvation Army is a church. We began to think

they thought we were the Boy Scouts and the Red Cross rolled into one. We have a lot of work to do because perceptions have an effect on recruitment. People aren't going to join an organization that looks quaint and old-fashioned. It also affects funding, because people aren't going to give their money in any substantial way to an organization that seems outdated and rather unsophisticated.

'Moreover, we're not as visible as we used to be. In Britain the Army's been around for such a long time that I think we've become part of the scenery and people don't take any notice of us any more. And they tend to think that we're not doing anything new, whereas in actual fact there is always something breaking out. What are we going to do about it? Well, we have commissioned an independent study that will look at our public image. One item that has leaked out, so I don't mind discussing it, is the question of uniform, and it seems that the general public wants the Salvation Army to retain its uniform. There are Salvationists who think we should become invisible, but the general public doesn't want us to be invisible. But they do think we look quaint and they do think we are Victorian, and that we are do-gooders and amateurs – none of which is true! Our social work is sophisticated and as good as anybody's. We've got lots of faults but we're not as quaint as people think we are. We must try to correct that.'

The decline both in the public perception of the Salvation Army and, more ominously, in the numbers of those proclaiming an allegiance to the church has been going on since the 1930s, Gowans said, yet it is far from universal. In countries such as Indonesia and post-Communist Russia, the Army is enjoying considerable growth. But the overall decline is irrefutable: in 1947 it could count on 124,000 soldiers; today there are only 43,000.

Sound advice from captain to cadet.

'Why is that? Well, it may be because of all those reasons I've just talked about. But I don't think we have recruited very vigorously either. We've been rather content to meander along and not make any serious efforts to recruit. I mean, when did you last see an advertisement in the newspapers saying, "Wouldn't you like to join the Salvation Army?" We're in decline to the same degree as some other churches. But that's cold comfort, isn't it? I do believe it has a lot to do with image and the fact that we never talked about ourselves. We're the best kept secret in the world, I think. People say they love the Salvation Army, but if you ask them what the Salvation Army is, or believes, or does, there's an ominous silence, because they don't have a very clear idea. So we've got to address that.'

It seems plausible to suggest that part of the reason for the Army's decline may be related to the success of other evangelical churches and movements, especially those with a more charismatic approach and a greater willingness to co-opt popular culture in the service of preaching and conversion. Gowans observed: 'Who can be sorry about that? Certainly not us! The others imitate us, that's all. If you go to Holy Trinity, Brompton, in central London, you'll find a typical old-style Salvation Army meeting, with very noisy chorus singing and participation. It seems that every blessed church in the kingdom now brings in a brass band to accompany its services. They

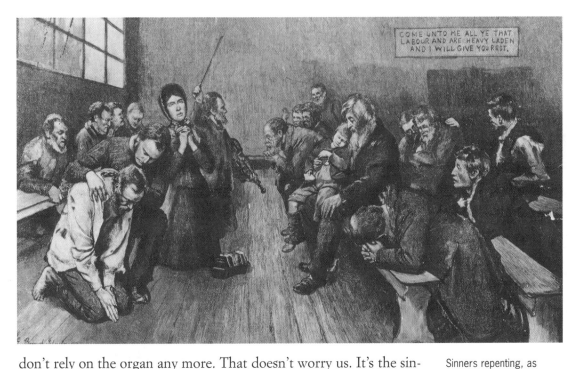

COME UNTO ME ALL YE THAT
LABOUR AND ARE HEAVY LADEN
AND I WILL GIVE YOU REST.

don't rely on the organ any more. That doesn't worry us. It's the sincerest form of flattery. And the need for the Gospel to be understood and communicated is big enough for all of us to engage in it, and anyone who is engaged seriously in it is our brother and our sister, whatever their denomination. In fact, I have always thought there were salvationists with a small 's' in all denominations. If you go to Paris and want to see a religious open-air prayer meeting, you have to choose between the Salvation Army and the Catholics. As for other evangelist churches, there are always flavours of the month that come and go. Listen, ninety per cent of the English population don't go to any church at all, so there's still plenty of room for us. Anyway, I'm a great believer in what I call the varied menu, different ways of communicating the message. Within the Salvation Army we also have different flavours, from the more sedate to the less organized. The freedom of a Salvation Army officer to lead any kind of meeting he likes is almost unlimited. I was in charge of a church for sixteen years and nobody ever told me what to do. There is no liturgy, there is no structure, you do whatever you like.'

Sinners repenting, as sketched in the 1890s.

161

Soldiers in uniform

Salvationists are proud of their instantly recognisable uniforms, but few would regret the passing of these tunics and bonnets, as worn between 1890 and 1930.

Possibly, I suggested, the very absence of liturgy and structure, as well as the inevitable diversity between churches and meetings, projected an image of inconsistency. To an outsider listening in, the theological message came over as a monotone of praising God and asking for His blessings and so forth. This was worthy but unsustaining on an intellectual level.

'I would hope,' Gowans replied, 'that the Salvation Army, in its conviction that it must be relevant and contemporary and young and noisy, doesn't lose that side of the Army that is meditative and profound. I can't help regretting what seems to be the decline in what were always called holiness meetings, the morning service on Sunday when the band only accompanied the first song and the meeting was meditative, when we expounded spiritual truths at a very profound level. It was never more than an hour, you didn't clap your hands, it was quiet. If I ask myself why I'm a Salvationist, it's because of those holiness meetings. The afternoon meeting tended to be noisy, and was called the Free and Easy because people came and went. The evening meeting was an outreach meeting when we tried to get sinners in and convert them. They offered three very different styles of meeting. The holiness meeting was, in my view, one of the pillars of the Army, and if we don't look after that side of our activities, we'll just be a frothy, noisy, only temporarily successful Salvation Army. Despite all appearance to the contrary, the Salvation Army is not just about saving souls but about making saints, and it is that aspect that is in danger of being lost in our evangelical excitements.

'One of the things I have always done is to go round to different meetings and listen to the preaching, which is terribly important. I like to know what kind of food is being presented on the table of the Lord on Sundays, and it's true that sometimes I am not pleased with the quality of what is being taught. It's superficial, it's trying too hard to catch the ear. You've got to do more than that. Once you've got the ear you've got to pour something into it. But often I'm pleasantly surprised too.'

Although the recently commissioned survey had shown that most people realize that the Salvation Army is primarily a church and not a social-welfare organization, there has always been a profound connection between the business of helping people and that of saving souls. Where should the boundary lie between the two?

'If sometimes we give the impression that if it weren't for saving souls we wouldn't be in social work, that would not be strictly true, because we are Christian people. Christ went about preaching his Gospel but also feeding the hungry and looking after the sick. He didn't say, "Now I am going to look after you because you're sick and afterwards you're going to be one of my disciples, aren't you?" His motive was not to convey his message in the narrow sense. He healed the sick because they were sick and he fed the hungry because they were hungry, and the Salvation Army, being Christian, is motivated in a similar way. But if at the same time we can convey the charity, the gentleness, the compassion of Christ, then we have in one way or another transmitted our message. We have demonstrated it, and that is where the spiritual side of our work comes in. If you speak to our clients I think they will tell you that we do not batter them on the head with the Bible, but they are impressed by the genuine concern. Whether they are consciously saved or not, they are receiving messages and indications that are not narrowly spiritual.'

But the Territorial Commander would be keen to see a spiritual as well as numerical revival within the Army. 'I'd like to see more attention given to the depths of spirituality in the Salvation Army. We're still seen as a theological lightweight in many areas, and quite unjustly, because for true Salvationists there is a very serious and deep side. There is a serious attempt being made now to offer more training. Things come in circles. In the early days the soldiers were trained. You didn't sign on the dotted line and that was it. There was a weekly soldiers' meeting where training was offered on spiritual life, on evangelism, on hygiene and all kinds of things. You were instructed on how to live, how to react to situations you were confronted with. If you were to come back in ten years' time, I would hope that the ongoing training of the Salvationists would be very much in place again, expanding not just their knowledge of the Bible, but their knowledge of Christian history, of Army history, of evangelism.'

The Army often seemed hampered by the rigidity of its structure. Time and again, I had encountered officers who longed to have more time to complete the work they had begun at their corps or social-service centre. While it was plausible to argue that a diversity of experience was beneficial, and that it was essential to avoid allowing officers to become too rooted or complacent by keeping them in the same job for too long, it could be argued that the lack of continuity was damaging organizationally as well as personally frustrating, and that this was compounded by the way in which the Army still appears to revel in secrecy, in the high drama of the sealed envelope.

'It's related to our history. The mobility of the Salvation Army was very important and the idea that people would be ready to go anywhere at any time without much notice gave the Army tremendous strength. But the idea that it's all done suddenly and without consultation is less and less true. What appears to fall out of the blue has had quite a lot of discussion. There are leaders who still prefer the old system. This is one way in which they can still show their authority. But less and less is that true. When I was young we were given ten days to move from one place to another. So the system isn't quite as autocratic as it seems. But the structure is still there, and perhaps the structure needs to be modified.'

John Gowans is receptive to the idea of change, if only because it is essential to halt the decline of the Army. 'I think we are at a crossroads. People have reached the stage where they have watched this gentle decline and say, "It's no good, we can't go on like this, obviously we need to change, obviously we're doing something wrong," and we're ready for it. Not totally, perhaps there's a two thirds majority in favour among the Army. These are critical dates. If we get it right now, we could have a very interesting future. If we don't get it right now, then what you see will continue, and gradually our influence will decline.'

There are a number of changes he favours. 'Some things would be very visible. One is a very much less military uniform, a more colourful and much cheaper uniform. I'm not a uniform person. I'm not regimented and organized, I don't like being structured as rigidly as a military system seems to suggest. I don't like it. But I do see the importance of having a visible church. I still see us in uniform, but a much more casual one, a much more pleasant one. The darkness of the Salvation Army uniform when you get us all together is depressing. How did we get to that? It's terrifying. But it depends where you are. When I was in Australia, we wore white mostly. In some parts of Africa it's grey. But in England we're still navy blue, very close to black.

'And it's incredible that some women still wear the bonnets. If anyone had told me forty years ago that some people would still be wearing bonnets as a kind of rearguard action … And yet we've brought out a rule just this week that is already creating a bit of a stir, that women Salvationists don't need to wear their hats inside the building. Never mind the bonnets, they don't even have to wear their hats if they don't want to! To come into a Salvation Army building and see all these people dressed in navy blue, with these helmets on, is very intimidating for a stranger.' (In an interview published in *The Times* a few weeks after I spoke to Commissioner Gowans, he was equally outspoken: 'I would love to see epaulettes go. And we must demolish the idea that the commissioner clicks his fingers and everybody does what he says. We realize that if we play the dinosaur, we are going to become extinct.')

'But these are superficial things. I'd like to see the present movement towards a variety of corps much more developed, and in ten years' time I think it will be. I hope in ten years when someone asks me to show them a typical Army corps to be able to say, "I'm sorry, but we haven't got one, there are hardly two of them alike, because they're adapting their programmes and their meetings and their worship sessions to the needs of the place where they are." We discovered long ago that what goes down well in, say, Bath won't go down well in Birmingham. Officers have always had enormous discretion, but they haven't used it! I've been in the business a long time, but I've always used my imagination and tried to do things a little differently, and nobody has ever corrected me or told me I couldn't do something, though sometimes they thought I was a bit crazy.

Commissioner John Gowans and his wife attend Sunday worship at Southwark corps.

'The message I am trying to get across is this. I once suggested to the editor of *The Salvationist* that we put just two words on the cover: "You Can". I'm fed up with people saying: "If only we could ..." Because you can! Possess your possessions! You've got liberty – use it! And what I've been saying since I came back to this country almost a year ago from Australia is: "Why are you not trying? Because you've got the liberty. And where they're using the liberty, it's tending to work."'

Cajoling, however, is not sufficient to bring about major changes within such a huge organization. For instance, Commissioner Gowans seems sympathetic to the idea of modifying the rule by which officers may only marry other officers if they wish to retain their commission. But he cannot make such a radical change to the rules unilaterally.

'The Salvation Army's richness is its internationalism but it's also its handicap. Here in Britain we might have no difficulty at all in introducing the individualism of the officer so far as their marriage is concerned, but when you talk internationally, as we do quite regularly, you find it doesn't fit with what, say, the Indians or Indonesians want. One of the things I push for is what I call territorial discretion but not everybody is in favour of that. For instance, we have rules for handling divorce questions in the Army. Here, too, the Indians don't want to know about it. So the wish to maintain a uniform front internationally makes for all kinds of difficulties. But the recognition of the woman officer as having her own gifts is now coming back. So we're saying, "She may be married to this twit but she's a clever lady, therefore we're going to give her a very important position and he will take something less significant," whereas the appointments of the couple, when I was young, used to depend on the qualities, or lack of them, of the husband. That way we often wasted the considerable talents of the officer wife.

'How do you bring changes about? You argue. When I was young, I assumed the commissioner could do what he liked. It's not quite like that. I can say my piece, and I'm invited to, but at the end of the day my bosses have the final say. It's still true at my level, and

I've been forty-three years in the Army, that I can't make appointments which are significant within my command entirely on my own. As for changing things, it does tend to be the international leaders' conference that sways things, because the General can do what he likes. Even things he says in election speeches are not binding. He can do something totally different once he's in power. So we have to convince him. But when he listens to the international leaders' conference, which takes place every two years or so, then he has to decide on what is best for the Army. Some of the changes will happen and some of them won't. But there is a very strong conservative streak in the Army.'

While pushing for the changes that he feels are necessary for the continuing vitality and effectiveness of the Salvation Army, John Gowans has to make sure that he keeps everyone on board.

'My job is to harmonize, to keep the thing together, not to allow things to polarize. There are those going enthusiastically, maybe over-enthusiastically, for change, perhaps for change's sake, and there are those who want to see things stay exactly as they always were. I plead with both sides to be more accepting of the other's point of view. You can understand that someone who has spent fifty years in one pattern finds it very difficult to accept change, and we have to have respect for what they have achieved. With the traditionalists I talk about the necessity to adapt to present needs and to find out what works. So I'm in the middle and get hit by traffic from both directions. I think we can change quite rapidly and quite radically without losing all the people we have. We have to have lots of talk and attempts to find common ground. But even the oldest, dyed-in-the-wool Salvationists, when challenged, will admit that what the Salvation Army is about is saving souls and caring for people, and it's not doing either of those very well right now. Incidentally, it's not a matter of age, of young and old. You can go to some corps and the people wearing the bonnets are the young ones. It's absolutely ridiculous and I tell them so. That's what makes me despair a little. You think the oldies will die off and the young ones will come forward, but often they're replaced by people with the same kind of narrow, traditional view.'

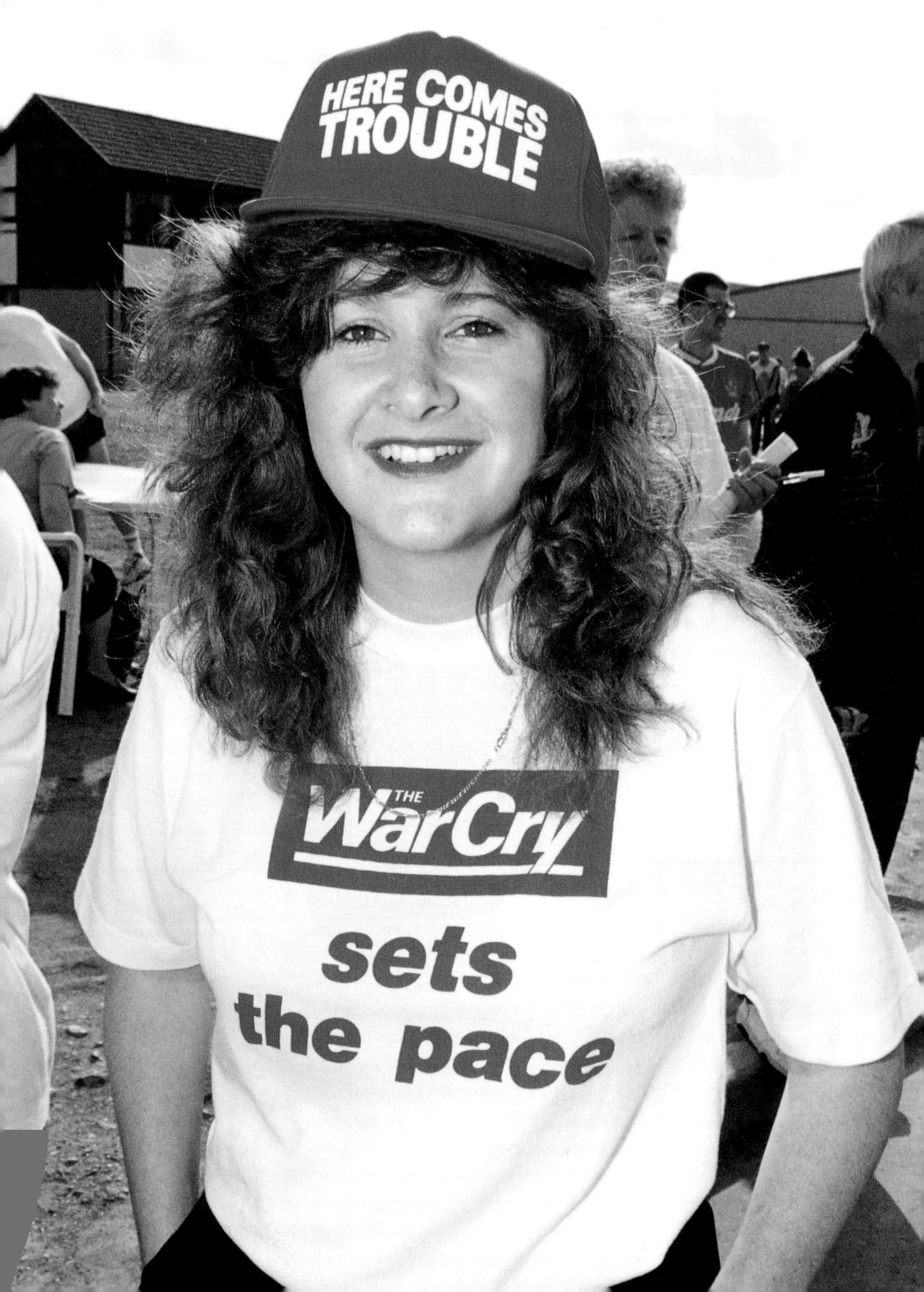
HERE COMES
TROUBLE
THE
WarCry
sets
the pace

8

The way forward

THE UPPER ECHELONS OF THE SALVATION ARMY, clearly troubled by the slow but inexorable decline of the church, have responded as large organizations usually do. They have commissioned studies and set up action groups. It was an American, Terry Camsey, then head of the church growth department at the London headquarters of the Army, who first suggested setting up a group that would deal with what Colonel Douglas Davis, the Chief Secretary of the British territory and thus the second-in-command, calls 'the re-imagining of ourselves'.

The outcome was the founding of the Vision Action Group under Colonel Davis's chairmanship. It is also known as the 20/20 Action group, since its brief is to look ahead at least twenty years into the future of the Army. Its purpose is to establish long-term goals for the Salvation Army rather than focus on short-term planning. 'It recognizes,' said Colonel Davis, 'the need to refocus and to take a holistic view of our ministry. But it's not enough to have a global vision of where we're going,' he argued. 'We need movers and shakers from the grass roots to come together and help us.' The group meets about three times a year and deliberately includes a majority of non-officers. One officer in the group is among the few who has succeeded in starting a new corps from scratch.

While continuing its deliberations, the group has issued an interim document called the 'Milestone 2002 Vision'. This is divided

Out goes the bonnet, in comes the baseball cap. A young Salvationist at Butlin's holiday camp in 1991.

into two sections: 'Key Elements' and 'Vision Objectives'. The former identifies the specific nature of the Army's sense of mission under such headings as 'Complete Knowledge of Jesus Christ', 'Fight for Social Justice', 'Actively Serve the Community,' and 'Spirit-filled Movement'. Vision Objectives sets out specific goals: for example, under 'Growing Movement' it is hoped that 'Through a commitment to evangelism there will be a 5 per cent increase in the "net" numbers of members each year.' Another states: 'We will improve our ability to win people to Christ by ensuring a minimum of 10 per cent a year of every corps congregation is trained in 1:1 evangelism.' On the social-service side: 'We will improve our ability to support people in need. Each Army centre will ensure its people have ready access to relevant local and national resources by 31 March 1999.'

And so it goes on. What seems to be lacking is any clear notion about how these objectives are to be achieved, though no doubt the Action Group will have given that matter serious thought too. In any event, Colonel Davis, as its chairman, feels reasonably sure that the decline in membership has bottomed out. Neither, he pointed out, is the Salvation Army the only church with this problem: the Methodist and Roman Catholic churches are experiencing the same phenomenon. The long-term solution, as he sees it, is to keep 'planting': in Army terminology, to found new corps wherever there seems to be a need.

For Simon Perkin, the newly commissioned officer, the key to growth is keeping young married couples within the church. 'I see the Army as a lifeboat, with plenty of room and activities for small children and for women. But less so for men. In my view, if you get the man, you get the family. We must persuade the men in the church to seek the fellowship of other men. But, of course, the problem is that there are so many distractions for young men and for couples.'

One clear consequence of the decline in officers within the Army has been the increasing use of lay workers to run Army agencies or centres. Phil Wall of Mission Team, who has a high profile within the church, is not an officer, and neither are the directors of Greig House or the Bristol Social Service Centre. It is not a contentious issue, as there is widespread recognition in the Army that it should hire the best people to do particular jobs, regardless of whether they are officers. In any case, all managers of Army service or outreach centres are committed Christians. Yet as the use of lay workers grows, as it inevitably will, the special Salvation Army identity of some centres may become diluted. That, at any rate, is the fear expressed, although I see little evidence for it.

John Gowans did not feel that the evangelical and charismatic churches that have been gaining in popularity constituted a threat to the health of the Salvation Army, and Colonel Davis took the same view, but with a more sceptical spin. 'It does appear that people who go to those kinds of churches shop around, moving from one to another. The question then arises as to how genuine those conversions are. Are those churches really reaching new people? People who adhere to the Salvation Army do so for other reasons, as it has a strong image of its own, and it makes a point of approaching those who would not normally have access to Christian teaching. Preaching on the streets on Sunday afternoons, our outdoor ministry, is one distinctive way in which the Army draws in new recruits. That's part of our history and it will continue. But we are also looking at other ways of bringing people into the fold of our church, such as parent and toddlers groups. The motto is: "Belong, then believe." More and more of the city-centre churches are keeping their doors open much longer during the day, so that people can wander in, whether it's to sit down for a few minutes after shopping, or whether it's to pray or seek advice.'

Captain Anne Read of Winton is also untroubled by 'competition' from other evangelical churches. Indeed, she is pleased if other churches have borrowed the Salvation Army's ideas. Moreover, she is happy to take a leaf or two from their books. Holy Trinity, Brompton, in central London, has developed a teaching course on Christianity called the Alpha Course, which she sees as a 'friendly way' to approach Bible teaching; it has been used successfully at Winton as well as at Notting Hill and many other corps. There is nothing wrong, she feels, in exchanging ideas and techniques.

As for the major problems faced by the Army, such as the decline in membership, Anne Read and others at corps level are confident that they are being addressed by the leadership. Anne cited, as had Commissioner Gowans, the need to secure international agreement before any significant change can come about, but she added: 'There are signs that God isn't finished with us.'

Others in the Salvation Army feel that it must regenerate itself from within as well as carry its ministry into the world at large. In 1990 Phil Wall was asked to work with the youth department of the Army, and began to travel the country, organizing communications programmes. Soon he was heading a mostly youthful evangelical team that in 1994 became formally recognized as the Mission Team, a movement that today enjoys a fervent, if far from universal, following within the Army. The crusading, evangelical, radical style of the Mission Team has not always found favour with the more conservative elements of the Army. There is also some resentment from officers that a non-officer such as Wall should have been entrusted with a budget that, after decades of service, they can only dream of. None the less the Team has the full support of Salvation Army headquarters.

Phil Wall of Mission Team, relaxing in his office.

Phil Wall was born into an Army family – 'I often say I was a foetal Salvationist' – but was not drawn to the Salvationist way of life. At the age of sixteen he left home, became a police cadet and remained in the force for eight years. When he was twenty he had various conversations that led to his acceptance of scripture and the Christian faith. At this time he was a riot squad officer, involved in such front-line police duties as dealing with the controversial miners' strike of 1984, and was also a keen boxer. He now realizes that he was living in an aggressive and even violent culture. As his faith grew, he saw that being a follower of Christ was hard to reconcile with this. He believed in law and order, and still does, yet now understands that he did not always make the right decisions when policing. 'But I wasn't quite Attila the Hun!' However, as he was confronted more and more with people who were living an overtly Christian life, he saw the contrast with his own way of life, which he resolved to bring more into line with his Christian ideals. Despite his image as something of an evangelical bruiser, Phil likes to think hard about what he is doing, and spent two years at theological college refining his Christian views. 'I do what I do because I love Jesus and I believe I'm doing the things he wants me to do. That's it. Simple.'

Like his older sister Julia, he eventually came back to the Salvationist fold. 'I returned to the Army partly because I was born into it, but it has also become a passion. The Army believes in meeting the needs of the whole man, with body, mind and spirit. I'm committed to that and want to see that happening with millions of people around the world. But the Army also concerns itself with injustice, with those who can't always speak up for themselves. One of the reasons I love the Salvation Army is that it's very public. We do what we do because the good news of the Christian faith is a public thing too, designed to impact on every aspect of life. I believe passionately in the Salvation Army. I do believe that we can change the world, just as our early leaders did. If I were to try to create an organization from scratch, it would end up looking something like the Salvation Army. Some people say that what we are doing with the Mission Team is not true to the traditions of the Salvation Army, but I'd like to sit them down and talk that through. The Mission Team may not look like the Salvation Army, but the substance is the same. The main difference between us and the mainstream Salvation Army is one of style rather than ethos. The Army is all about pragmatism, about doing everything we can to communicate with people. I'd like to see us being as effective, perhaps even more effective, than Booth was. That's my dream.'

The Mission Team's motto is 'Reaching the Unreached, Training the Untrained'. Its own brochure states: 'Our purpose is to facilitate effective mission within the UK territory. Since September 1990 we have been involved in mission throughout the Salvation Army in the UK. This work takes place in all kinds of situations from local missions at corps to national training initiatives. If you're interested in being better equipped for mission, wherever you are and whatever you are doing, why not see what you can do with the Mission Team?'

This Scottish old-age pensioner is determined to get to his feet unaided. An officer stands by, just in case.

There is a sense in which Mission Team has developed into a personality cult, though it would be unfair to accuse Phil of having sought that. He is a large, powerfully built man – you can see why the police force was keen to have him – with small, dark, intense eyes and a dynamism that pervades everything he does.

Some members of the Mission Team attest to his charismatic leadership, exclaiming: 'He is such a great man of God, such a good bloke to be with … He's a passionate man and he believes passionately in what he's doing. Sometimes he gets a bit too excited and we have to pull him back down to the ground!' Phil Wall admits that he has made mistakes. Moreover, he recognizes that when an older generation of Salvationists has worked hard to do their best for the movement in their own way, 'when you come in and try and pioneer something new, by definition those people feel marginalized and debased. We do get hassle, we get opposition and challenges, but most people are very supportive, or at least happy that we're around and trying to do what we do. Some people imagine that we're somehow anti-Salvation Army, not committed to it – which is a total myth. We are deeply committed to the Salvation Army, it is our only passion, our only vision. But because what we do is a threat to some of the existing processes and methods, people react to that, sometimes very strongly. We, and I in particular, will need to be more sensitive to that at times, but the bottom line is that who we are today isn't matching the needs of today and tomorrow. We need to say, "Let's hold on to what's good and improve what's good to make it better, but let's let go of those things that have been dead for some time."'

However, an old-timer such as Mrs Chase at Notting Hill, without mentioning Mission Team or its revivalist weekends known as Roots, was uneasy about what she perceives as new ideas coursing through the Army: 'I don't agree with some of what they are doing, the younger people. I think it's going to ruin the Salvation Army, actually. There have to be changes, but not some of the changes that they're thinking about doing. I prefer it as it was, you know, I'm the old-fashioned type. But I'd never leave the Army, never.'

When the upper echelons of the Army speak of movers and shakers at the grass-roots level, they may well have in mind men like Phil Wall. Despite the important position he holds within the Army, he is an employee and not an officer. 'I'm interested in leverage and influence, not in hierarchy,' he explained, 'but if at some point I felt the call, then I would consider becoming an officer. But at present I feel I can have greater influence by not being commissioned.' So in the meantime he is an enthusiastic soldier at his local corps in Raynes Park.

The Mission Team considers itself militant in its commitment to Christianity, and Phil believes its values are identical to those of the Salvation Army at large, even though it is composed of younger people and expresses its values in a different style. It differs from the conventional Army outreach programmes in steering clear of soup kitchens or mobile canteens, but on the other hand it has become actively involved in programmes designed to help Aids sufferers. What makes it distinctive from other Army groups is that it uses mixed media – drama, videos and music – to communicate the message of the gospel. The Team, which is based in rather scruffy offices in Morden in South London, runs an evangelism training course, a one-year arts programme, and publishes a quarterly magazine. It also conceived and organizes the celebratory evangelical Roots weekends, which seek to instil new energy and commitment into Salvationists.

The Mission Team's most distinctive innovation is probably the programme known as Hope 10/10. It arose out of an attempt by Phil and his wife Wendy to adopt a child while they were in South Africa. For various reasons it did not work out, so with the grandiose thinking that seems second nature to him, he said to his wife, 'Well, if we can't adopt this one child personally, let's try and adopt the whole lot, all hundred of them, financially.' At Ethembeni, a Salvation Army children's home in Johannesburg, the Army cares for children born HIV-positive until they are four. Many develop Aids and die long before they reach that age. These sick children need a great deal of care, and the Hope 10/10 programme plans to raise £1 million over the next two years to develop two homes, staff them

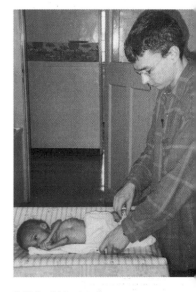

British athlete Jonathan Edwards helps out at the Ethembeni orphanage for HIV-positive children in Johannesburg.

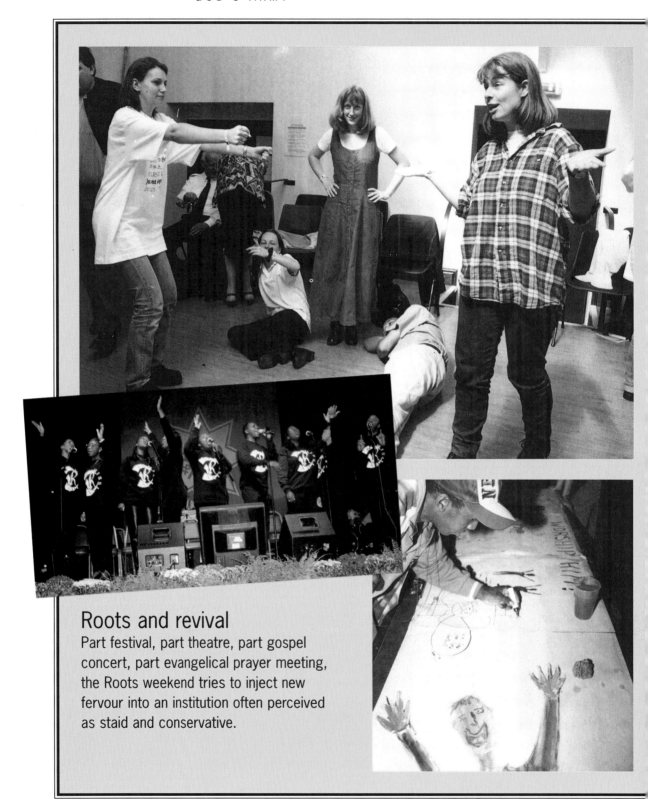

Roots and revival

Part festival, part theatre, part gospel concert, part evangelical prayer meeting, the Roots weekend tries to inject new fervour into an institution often perceived as staid and conservative.

with trained nurses and equip them with medical facilities. Phil has enlisted the patronage of the British athlete Jonathan Edwards, who has visited Ethembeni and admires the work that takes place there.

What is unusual about Hope 10/10 is its means of fundraising. Anyone who wishes to participate is handed ten pounds. They are asked either to return it (if they can't think of what to do with it), or to hang on to it (if they feel they need it badly themselves), or to put it to work in some way that will help it grow substantially. The Mission Team suggests various ways in which the money can be put to use: for example, it can be spent on provisions for a barbecue for which an admission fee is collected, or on a sponsored walk or silence, and so on. According to Phil and Janet Waterton, co-ordinators of the scheme and members of the Mission Team, some enterprising people have made the money grow tenfold, even hundredfold, before returning it to the Hope 10/10 account. Phil accepts that they may lose up to 5 per cent of the money they give out, but they will earn far more. There is, of course, a spiritual and ideological motivation behind Hope 10/10, which Phil Wall defines as follows: 'It gives us a way of showing that we are not just communicators of the Word, but doers of the Word too. It's not enough to proclaim our Christianity. We have to live it too.' In the spring of 1998 Hope 10/10 was also launched in Canada, and Phil is doing his best to interest the business and media communities in the project.

Nevertheless the main thrust of the Mission team is revivalist. 'We are passionately evangelical and want to communicate that,' Phil insisted. 'We want to be Good News people. We are thankful to God and to the Army as a whole for trusting the Mission team. The Salvation Army has achieved great things in the past, but we feel we're just getting started, that our best days as an organization are still ahead of us. Incidentally, it isn't true that the Mission Team only works with young people. Nor is it true that we are mavericks. We are radical only in the sense that we believe in going back to the roots, we believe in renaissance. But in no way are we working against the Salvation Army. I have certainly made mistakes but I am completely loyal to the organization. I admire our leaders, especially John

Gowans. He accepts his responsibilities, his heart is in the right place, and he is passionate about the future of the Army. Sometimes he has taken a lot of flak on my behalf. He's encouraged us, inspired us, stood with us. I personally have no problem with authority – just remember that I was a policeman. So it's a myth that the Mission Team is out on a limb. The last thing the Salvation Army needs is a loud-mouthed idiot in my position going off on his own. It's true I was as arrogant as could be when I was a young evangelist. I'm not like that any more. I hope I'm wiser, but I'm still just as intense when it comes to my faith.'

It is clear that Phil Wall has thought deeply about the persistent decline of the Salvation Army and sees the Mission Team as a force for internal renewal as well as spiritual outreach. 'The Salvation Army has been losing its intensity of passion and commitment and was hit badly by the two world wars. It can replicate the system it has set up but not the passion that used to drive it. To reverse the decline, we need to discover the essence of who we are. We've been slow to come to terms with the massive cultural changes within society. In the previous century the Army was in the forefront of engaging with the culture around it, but we haven't kept up. We have been selling out to the predominant value systems of our day, such as materialism, consumerism and individualism, making us less effective in what we do. We need to be distinctive again, morally, ethically, from those around us. To make this effective would force huge changes on the Army, as current leadership models are unhelpful, and not a model that Jesus would have wanted or that people want today.' He doesn't want the Army to be a mausoleum, and would sooner it died than see it preserved as a museum. 'The Salvation Army needs to be a living organism. If it doesn't change dramatically, we're dead as a dodo, and we'd need to start a new organization to get the job done. But that would take a hundred years!' He likes the analogy of the Army as a vast oil tanker that is slowly but surely heading off in the wrong direction and needs to be turned around. For the leadership to do so alone would take a few miles; the purpose of events such as Roots is to act as a tugboat to help turn it round within a few hundred yards.

Del may look like any other scruffy teenager in London but he's a mainstay of Southwark corps, where he is the lead guitarist.

'It's hard for a 120-year-old institution to accept change. Our goal isn't to reject the past, but we can't be sentimental. There has to be a reason for the Salvation Army to exist, and if so it needs to be effective. William Booth was a pragmatist. He believed that if it doesn't work, bin it. We may have stepped over the line sometimes and offended a few people, but the bottom line is that we are here to fulfil our role. And I'm convinced that the best years of the Army are still to come.

'People look at us and can't quite work out what we are and what we are about, so we need to relate better to our own communities. The Booths wanted the Army to be accessible, which is what the brass bands and uniforms were all about. But our culture has moved on, and we have to do whatever needs to be done to get the Good News out to people. So we try to communicate the Good News of Jesus in any way we can, to put forward the holistic message of Jesus, and also we want to equip and resource the Salvation Army. Roots is one way we're wrestling with those challenges.'

As its name suggests, Roots is an attempt to return Salvationism to its spiritual origins, to bring about spiritual renewal. Through it Phil Wall wants to bring back to the Salvation Army some qualities that are in danger of being lost: vision, passion, idealism, motivation. He wants to 'put the mission into the forefront of what we're about and to equip Salvationists to fulfil their mission mandate as best they can'. Behind the verbiage is a more radical agenda, a desire to change the sub-culture of the Salvation Army. Phil Wall is aware of the size of the task he has set himself: 'Many people in the Salvation Army have a lot invested in the status quo. So change is a challenge for them. But we have to face up to the fact that the Army in the UK has been declining for sixty years.'

Roots enjoys widespread support, even from Salvationists such as Captain Valerie Hope, who comes across as relatively conventional. She believes that Phil and his colleagues remain close to the original values of the Salvation Army, and she applauds their efforts to pull the Army from the rut into which it lapsed, she believes, in the 1930s. 'We often say that if William Booth was alive today he'd turn in his

grave. But Phil is much closer in his approach to Booth and the traditional Salvation Army.'

In many respects Roots is an evangelical festival, a kind of latter-day tent meeting, crammed with prayer sessions, rock concerts, group and family activities, seminars, children's entertainment and testimony. No such movement is complete without its mission statement, and Roots proclaims: 'Roots seeks to encourage spiritual renewal and to equip Salvationists for mission and evangelism.' Not everyone likes the radical evangelism that Roots represents, with its talk of miracles and the workings of the Holy Spirit, but the festival, and indeed the Mission Team's activities as a whole, have the blessing of the Army establishment.

Nothing could have made this clearer than Commissioner John Gowans's presence at the 1998 Roots weekend at Southport, and the presence of Commissioner Kay Rader, wife of the General, the year before. The theme of John Gowans's address, delivered with the same oratorical power as his sermons on Commissioning Day, is that the business of the Salvation Army has to be the saving of souls. 'We should be plotting and scheming, designing and praying, to get someone saved. We must think, What shall we do next to get to the unsaved? What can we do to win more souls? ...

'The Salvation Army means the total belief in the power of Jesus to save souls and in the power of the Holy Spirit to make soul-winners out of unlikely people. When someone who doesn't know Jesus sees Him in a living, walking, talking person, he is dumbfounded by it. When he sees integrity, honesty, total unselfishness and compassion, he is attracted to it like a magnet. The soul-winner must be Christ-like – otherwise he's repulsive, he repels. The whole strength of the Holy Spirit is at the disposition of everyone who wants to project in their ugly self something beautiful that is Christ.

'The question isn't "Are you a Salvationist and do you play in the band?" but "Are you a soul-winner? When did you last lead someone to Jesus?" The Salvation Army is a soul-winning machine in the hands of the Holy Spirit.'

PHIL WALL INSISTS that his job is to revitalize the Army, and he is entirely unconcerned with what he calls its structural challenges. That may be so, but he has thought deeply about the image that the Army has been projecting to the outside world, especially since the way the Army is perceived is inevitably bound up with its prospects for survival as the kind of crusading, evangelical, soul-saving church that everyone involved in it wants to see.

Take, for example, the military metaphor that pervades the Salvation Army: the hierarchical ranking of its officers and NCOs, the uniforms, the marching bands, the almost papal figure of an all-powerful General. It is not clear whether this military structure works to its advantage or otherwise. Certainly to me, the massed ranks of blue serge uniforms at Regent Hall detracted from the spiritual resonance of the meeting. Yet there are strong arguments for retaining the uniform: the market-research report published in 1998 seemed to show that the uniform was crucial to the identity of the Army in terms of its perception by the outside world. Captain Bill Cochrane, the Army's external-relations officer, described the uniform as a 'walking advert'. Others add that the uniform is a leveller that puts all members of the Army, whatever their background, on an equal footing.

'If we didn't have our uniform,' said Douglas Davis, the Chief Secretary, 'nobody would know what the Salvation Army was. So I'm quite sure we won't dispense with it, but I do think it's likely that we will modify it. Often when I'm travelling with my wife, and we're both in uniform, people who are complete strangers will come up to us and talk, and sometimes ask us to pray with them if they are troubled by something in their personal lives. That could never happen if we were not in uniform. And the other thing we have found is that many of the new recruits, especially in countries such as Australia, are enthusiastic about the uniform and want to wear it. And it isn't only the Salvation Army that adopts the military metaphor. Charismatics are always appealing to images of spiritual warfare. It's part of their language, the struggle between good and evil.'

Captain Len Ballantine, who conducts the International Staff Songsters, doesn't see how the Army can operate without its military-

They're always there!

The Salvation Army's instinct is to respond to need, wherever it occurs. Top: Distributing food, drink and clothing to victims of Hurricane Andrew in the United States in 1993. Above: Bringing refreshments to firemen at a blaze on London's Bread Street on 1995. Left: Taking a light-hearted view of its own constant readiness to help.

style approach. 'The Army knows it needs to be defined and ordered. To do our work we need a disciplined force. It's a choice people make. The Army tends to get you early and keep you – or it doesn't get you at all.'

For Phil Wall, 'The military side of the Salvation Army is a metaphor for our war against injustice, oppression. The uniform is not the substance, it's the metaphor. What differentiates us from other evangelical churches is not so much that we wear uniforms, though some of us do, but that we deal with the marginalized, wherever they are. I admit that others, such as Catholics, do exactly the same, especially in places like Africa. But in this country the average Salvationist doesn't come anywhere near the poor or the marginalized. Most Salvationists are professional people. Our challenge is to reactivate the body politic of the Salvation Army around the marginalized. Otherwise, what's the reason for our being? We could just as well be Baptists instead.'

However, Phil worries that a uniformed army no longer conveys a positive image to the outside world. 'The military image on which we are based is not a positive one. Ask people what they associate with uniforms and ranks, and they'll mention dictators and the impotence of the United Nations. Perhaps there's a more positive image associated with freedom fighters in some parts of the world. I like the military metaphor but not the military format, which is only a pragmatic response. The SAS is extremely effective without having uniforms. Our difficulty is that we look at the old Salvationist in her high-collar uniform and bonnet on a hot summer's day and our culture praises her for that steadfastness and loyalty. But the world looks at her and says, "Hey, lady, you're crazy." During the Boer War the British soldiers wore their scarlet uniforms, which looked splendid but also made them easy targets to pick off on the veldt. Their officers made them wear those uniforms out of stubbornness, but they were the wrong form for the context. We have to think in similar ways. We have to remember that it is the responsibility of the

The next generation of soldier decides that if the cap fits, she should wear it.

Salvation Army to adapt to the modern world. We can't expect the modern world and the general public to shape themselves according to our views.'

As so often happens when reform or change is in the air within a venerable organization, the most forceful opposition seems to come from outside the movement. As news of the possible changes in the Army uniform emerged, on 15 June 1998, the *Daily Telegraph* launched a fierce defence of the traditional view of the Salvation Army: 'Haven't they considered that the uniforms are precisely the reason why so many people take them seriously?' No doubt the men and women who have given their lives to the service of the Army will reach their own judicious conclusion, without the help of the more reactionary segments of the national press.

The uniform is just one part, the most visible, of the Army's sub-culture. But I told Phil Wall how struck I had been during the Commissioning Day ceremonies by the inwardness of the proceedings. For the outsider there were a multiplicity of codes to be absorbed and interpreted. At moments such as this, however impressive the ceremonies, there is something of the cult about the Salvation Army.

He immediately recognized what I was trying to say. 'Yes, it's like cocooning, a form of siege mentality. The Army does tremendous work in the world, but this cocooning has to do with the personal agendas of individuals. It's perfectly true that the Salvation Army has its own sub-culture. As an evangelical church it was designed to be totally accessible, but if you're not part of the organization you won't understand Salvation Army traditions and biblical imagery, or the peculiar language that we sometimes use, all of which militates against communication. So that comes back to my job, which is to turn things around. The core of what I do is the Bible, Jesus, our heritage. The Salvation Army is most powerful when it is engaged. As an organization it is morally and ethically distinct, but when it comes to people it needs to be culturally engaged. It's important that we relate to the culture around us, but that doesn't mean we need to assimilate it. The fact is that many of us still live just like our neighbours, only we're stuck in the nineteen-thirties format of the Salvation Army.'

For Captain Len Ballantine change is necessary but will only come from below. 'You can partly explain the decline in the Army's numbers by the fact that it demands a complete commitment. You are required to serve God through this institution. So it's cult-like, and it's hard to be free when you're so controlled. Of course, many people are trying to do something about this. But change will only come about at grass-roots level. Six years ago you would have seen the female cadets all wearing bonnets. It became a big issue, a question of identity. The problem often is that the laity is more conservative than the soldiers and officers. The bonnet or the uniform is their mantle of worship and it's hard to let go of it. It's clear that the insistence on officers only marrying other officers won't continue to work. It creates far too much tension.'

Phil Wall also thinks the Army will have to loosen its grip if the decline is to be halted. 'The Salvation Army celebrates uniformity when our culture is increasingly diverse and doesn't want anything prescribed to it. That's a massive challenge for us. We're not even asking these questions. Instead we're asking why people don't come to church. Our parents in the Salvation Army were trained to lead in a world that doesn't exist any more. If you'd asked my father to jump, he would ask, "How high?" I, and most people of my generation, and I'm thirty-four, want to know why we have to jump. We'll jump just as high as my father but we want to know what we're doing it for. There's a general shift to a more questioning world.

'My parents suffered a lot of abuse when they became Salvationists. Their families were furious and held them in contempt. So their faith cost them dear. All this suffering and loyalty is part of their inheritance. Yet we must not devalue their sacrifice by trying to protect some kind of outdated or outmoded system. We have a tendency in the Army sometimes to call sterility "faithfulness". We can't afford that kind of sentimentality. I have enormous respect for my parents and their generation and the sacrifices they made. But we do them no honour by living in the past.'

It seems inevitable that the more forward-looking leaders of the Salvation Army – and that includes Commissioner Gowans as well as Phil Wall and countless officers at corps level – are bound to have a struggle on their hands as they try to tug the Army into the twenty-first century. Like all venerable organizations, it is riddled with outdated practices that have ossified into 'traditions'. It is not for an outsider to decide which direction the Salvation Army should take both to guarantee its survival and maintain its distinctive identity. But it is an important debate, because whether one has sympathy or disdain for its evangelical message, this big-hearted organization deserves to live on.

INDEX

PICTURE SOURCES